Operation ENDURING FREEDOM

US Military Operations in Afghanistan, 2001-2002

By Lou Drendel

squadron/signal publications

(Previous Page) Two F-15E Strike Eagles flank a B-1B Lancer (aka 'Bone') while flying near Mountain Home Air Force Base (AFB), Idaho. Aircraft from the Mountain Home-based 366th Expeditionary Wing (EW) were deployed for missions over Afghanistan during Operation ENDURING FREEDOM. The F-15Es are assigned to the 391st Fighter Squadron (FS), while the B-1B is from the 34th Bomb Squadron (BS). (USAF)

Foreword

This is a pictorial record of the first six months of a war unlike any ever fought by American forces. Practically all of the images in this book are official photos, taken on the frontline of the American war on terror. Because the majority of the combat consisted of the application of air power, most of what you will see here are American strike aircraft. This enemy has a fragmented organizational structure, at best. It is an enemy from the Middle Ages, rooted in a culture that hates modernity and everything associated with human progress. It is solely dedicated to the death of its perceived enemies, but it is an enemy capable of using the tools of modernity against Western civilization. Their demonstration of this capability on one horrific September morning in 2001 provided the catalyst for Operation ENDURING FREEDOM. This operation continues as this book is written, with elite American and Allied ground forces focused on eliminating the remnants of the Afghan terrorist cadre.

A Legacy of Terror

Middle Eastern terrorists have a long history of attacks against Americans and American interests worldwide. Before 11 September 2001, the strikes had been either on foreign soil or relatively limited in scope. The deadliest such attacks were the 1983 bombing of a Marine barracks in Beirut, Lebanon, in which 242 Americans died, and the 1988 downing of Pan Am Flight 103 – a **Boeing 747** – over Lockerbie, Scotland, which killed 259 people. Assaults on the US homeland included the 1993 bombing of New York City's World Trade Center, which killed six and injured 1000. A lone Palestinian gunman fired on visitors to the Empire State Building in New York on 23 February 1997, killing one person and wounding four before killing himself.

Other notable terrorist attacks included the US Embassy bombings in Kenya and Tanzania on 7 August 1998, in which 291 died and approximately 5000 were injured. On 12 October 2000, an assault on the destroyer USS COLE (DDG-67) in Aden harbor, Yemen killed 17 sailors and wounded 39 others. Osama bin Laden – an expatriate Saudi national – was held responsible for both attacks. American response to all terrorist attacks was limited in scope and did little to discourage the continued planning and execution of terror attacks on civilians.

That all ended on 11 September 2001.

"...we calculated in advance the number of casualties from the enemy, who would be killed based on the position of the tower. We cal-

Saudi-born Osama bin Laden, leader of the al-Qaeda terrorist network, makes a videotaped statement from 'somewhere in Afghanistan.' Al-Qaeda was established in 1988 and was held responsible for the 11 September 2001 attacks on the United States.

ISBN 0-89747-443-0

If you have any photographs of aircraft, armor, soldiers or ships of any nation, particularly wartime snapshots, why not share them with us and help make Squadron/Signal's books all the more interesting and complete in the future. Any photograph sent to us will be copied and the original returned. The donor will be fully credited for any photos used. Please send them to:

Squadron/Signal Publications, Inc.
1115 Crowley Drive
Carrollton, TX 75011-5010

Если у вас есть фотографии самолетов, вооружения, солдат или кораблей любой страны, особенно, снимки времён войны, поделитесь с нами и помогите сделать новые книги издательства Эскадрон/Сигнал еще интереснее. Мы переснимем ваши фотографии и вернём оригиналы. Имена приславших снимки будут сопровождать все опубликованные фотографии. Пожалуйста, присылайте фотографии по адресу:

Squadron/Signal Publications, Inc.
1115 Crowley Drive
Carrollton, TX 75011-5010

軍用機、装甲車両、兵士、軍艦などの写真を所持しておられる方はいらっしゃいませんか？どの国のものでも結構です。作戦中に撮影されたものが特に良いのです。Squadron/Signal社の出版する刊行物において、このような写真は内容を一層充実し、興味深くすることができます。当方にお送り頂いた写真は、複写の後お返しいたします。出版物中に写真を使用した場合は、必ず提供者のお名前を明記させて頂きます。お写真は下記にご送付ください。

Squadron/Signal Publications, Inc.
1115 Crowley Drive
Carrollton, TX 75011-5010

culated that the floors that would be hit would be three or four floors. I was the most optimistic of them all...due to my experience in this field, I was thinking that the fire from the gas [aviation fuel] in the plane would melt the iron structure of the building and collapse the area where the plane hit and all the floors above it only. This is all that we had hoped for." **– Osama bin Laden**

At 0745 hours, Eastern Daylight Time (EDT), American Airlines Flight 11, a **Boeing 767** with 92 people on board, departed Boston's Logan International Airport, bound for Los Angeles. Among the passengers were Satam M.A. Al Suqami, Waleed M. Alshehri, Wail M. Alshehri, Mohamed Atta, and Abdulaziz Alomari. Four of these five men were believed to be pilots.

At 0758, United Airlines Flight 175, another Boeing 767 bound for Los Angeles, departed Boston with 65 people on board. Among those aboard were Marwan Al-Shehhi, Fayez Rashid Ahmed Hassan Al Qadi Banihammad, Ahmed Alghamdi, Hamza Alghamdi, and Mohand Alshehri.

At 0810, American Airlines Flight 77, a **Boeing 757** with 64 passengers, departed Washington's Dulles International Airport en route to Los Angeles. The passengers included Khalid Almihdhar, Hajed Moqed, Nawaf Alhazmi, Salem Alhazmi, and Hani Hanjour.

At 0842, United Airlines Flight 93, also a Boeing 757, left Newark International Airport bound for San Francisco with 45 passengers. Saeed Alghamdi, Ahmed Ibrahim A. Al Haznawi, Ahmed Alnami, and Ziad Samir Jarrah were aboard.

All four airliners were hijacked, apparently using nearly identical methods. The terrorists carried box cutter razor blades and used them to force their way into the cockpit. According to cell-phone calls made by other passengers during the hijackings, the hijackers killed flight attendants and pilots as they took control of the aircraft. They were able to do this because: a) box cutters were not prohibited carry-on items, and b) the then-accepted procedure during a hijacking was to accede to the demands of the hijackers in order to save the lives of everyone aboard.

These hijackers were not interested in saving any lives, including their own. They were focused on killing as many Americans as they possibly could, and at least those who were flying the airliners were willing to die in the commission of their crimes.

At 0845 hours, EDT, American Airlines Flight 11 crashed into the north side of the north tower of the World Trade Center in New York City. It struck the building between the 96th and 103rd floors. Occupants of the building began an immediate evacuation. Many people in the south tower began their own evacuation, although building officials in the south tower made announcements that evacuation was not necessary.

At 0903, United Airlines Flight 175, traveling at 584 MPH (939.8 KMH) – a speed that threatened the airframe's integrity – crashed into the south tower of the World Trade Center between the 87th and 93rd floors. It was immediately apparent that these were acts of terror and the US government acted quickly to prevent any further incidents.

At 0917 hours, EDT, the Federal Aviation Administration (FAA) shut down all New York City area airports.

At 0921, the Port Authority of New York and New Jersey ordered all bridges and tunnels in the New York area closed.

At 0924, President George W. Bush, speaking from a scheduled appearance in Florida, called the crashes into the World Trade Center *"a national tragedy."*

At 0934, the White House and the Capitol in Washington, DC were closed.

At 0940, United States airspace was cleared. No civilian aircraft were allowed to take off, all en route aircraft were instructed to land immediately at the nearest appropriate facility, and all international flights en route to the United States were diverted to Canada. The FAA announced that all commercial flights in the United States would be cancelled until at least noon the following day. It was the first time in history this had ever been done.

At 0943, American Airlines Flight 77 crashed into the west side of the Pentagon in Arlington, Virginia, just west of Washington. This killed 125 people in the building – headquarters of the US Department of Defense – and all aboard the aircraft. Passenger Barbara Olson had called her husband, Solicitor General Ted Olson, at 0925 to say the passengers and pilots were being held in the back of the aircraft.

At 1005, the World Trade Center's south tower collapsed. The intense fire started by exploding jet fuel had so weakened the steel support columns that they could not hold the weight of the floors above. Their collapse started a chain reaction, which caused all floors below to crash to the ground in a gigantic cloud of pulverized masonry.

At 1010, a section of the Pentagon collapsed. At the same time, United Airlines Flight 93 crashed into a field in Somerset County, in western Pennsylvania. Cell phone calls from passengers indicated they were aware of the attacks on the World Trade Center and that they were going to attempt to re-take the aircraft from the hijackers.

At 1029, the north tower of the World Trade Center collapsed in the same manner as the south tower.

While these events unfolded, the news wires were alive with rumors of additional attacks, ranging from car bombs to additional hijacked jumbo jets en route to Washington. The probable death toll was grossly exaggerated, as it was reported that up to 50,000 people could have been in the buildings when they were hit. (The final death toll was less than 3000.)

The President was aboard Air Force One[1], destination unknown. Disaster plans were implemented. The United Nations building in New York was evacuated and New York Mayor Rudy Giuliani ordered the evacuation of lower Manhattan. **F-15 Eagle** and **F-16 Fighting Falcon** fighters began patrolling the skies over major cities, with orders to shoot down any intruders. Washington's mayor declared a state of emergency, the National Guard was called out, and the President put the US military on the highest state of alert.

[1] Air Force One is the call sign of a US Air Force aircraft that the President is aboard. This is usually given to one of two Boeing **VC-25As**, extensively modified versions of the **Boeing 747-200B** airliner.

At 1720 hours, the 47-story World Trade Center Building 7 collapsed due to fire and damage sustained when the twin towers collapsed.

Afghanistan became the immediate focus of attention with a report of explosions and tracer fire over the capitol city, Kabul. The US denied any responsibility for these events, but it was clear that the Taliban-controlled Afghanistan was viewed as a state that sponsored terrorism openly. It was also clear that the al-Qaeda[2] network, harbored by the Taliban[3] and controlled by Osama bin Laden, would be a prime suspect in the investigation of these attacks.

Much has been written about the failure of intelligence to predict the events of 11 September 2001. In fact, the Central Intelligence Agency (CIA) had been warning Congress and the public of the danger of ignoring the growing threat posed by al-Qaeda. CIA Director George J. Tenet had issued the following warnings:

28 January 1998, Senate Select Committee on Intelligence (SSCI) hearing: *"There has been a trend toward increasing lethality of attacks, especially against civilian targets. A confluence of recent developments increases the risk that individuals or groups will attack US interests."*

2 February 1999, Senate Armed Services Committee hearing: *"...there is not the slightest doubt that Usama [sic] bin Laden, his worldwide allies, and his sympathizers are planning further attacks against us."*

18 October 1999, Georgetown University lecture: *"You need go no further than Usama bin Laden – the perpetrator of the East Africa bombings. He has declared the acquisition of weapons of mass destruction a religious duty and identified every American as a legitimate target."*

2 February 2000, SSCI hearing: *"Usama bin Laden is still foremost among these terrorists, because of the immediacy and seriousness of the threat he poses. Everything we have learned recently confirms our conviction that he wants to strike further blows against America. Despite some well-publicized disruptions, we believe he could still strike without additional warning."*

7 February 2001, SSCI hearing: *"Usama bin Laden and his global network of lieutenants and associates remain the most immediate and serious threat. Since 1998, Bin Laden has declared all US citizens legitimate targets of attack. His organization is continuing to place emphasis on developing surrogates to carry out attacks in an effort to avoid detection, blame, and retaliation. The Taliban shows no sign of relinquishing terrorist Usama Bin Laden, despite strengthened UN sanctions and prospects that Bin Laden's terrorist operations could lead to retaliatory strikes against Afghanistan."*

The information that prompted these warnings came from sources worldwide. An example of this was the arrest of Abdul Hakim Murad

[2] Al-Qaeda is Arabic for 'the base.'

[3] Taliban is Pashto for 'students.' Islamic seminary students made up the original Taliban organization.

Afghanistan's Taliban government was among the most oppressive in history. The regime imposed a strict interpretation of the Koran – Islam's holy book – which included a ban on music and no education for women and girls. Their military wore traditional garb and were primarily armed with Russian weapons, including the Rocket Propelled Grenade (RPG) carried by one of these soldiers.

Afghanistan became the focal point of Operation ENDURING FREEDOM. Although it is land-locked, most of its neighbors cooperated – actively or passively – with the US-led coalition. This coalition began attacking Taliban and al-Qaeda positions in Afghanistan on 7 October 2001.

Afghanistan

————	International boundary
– – –	Province (velāyat) boundary
★	National capital
◎	Province (velāyat) capital
+–+–+	Railroad
————	Road

The existence of two new provinces of Nurestan and Khowst has not been confirmed.

| 0 | 100 | 200 Kilometers |
| 0 | 100 | 200 Miles |

Lambert Conformal Conic Projection, SP 25 N / 39 N

surprise to everyone in the United States. The fact that American investigators were able to pinpoint the source of the attacks so quickly confirmed that ample evidence existed pointing straight at Afghanistan and Osama bin Laden. If the attacks themselves were a big surprise to most Americans, the American response to these strikes may have been an even bigger surprise to the Taliban and to al-Qaeda. After eight years of the Clinton administration's equivocal and ineffectual response to terror, bin Laden was now up against a considerably different adversary.

America Strikes Back

"And tonight, the United States of America makes the following demands on the Taliban: Deliver to United States authorities all the leaders of al-Qaeda who hide in your land. Release all foreign nationals, including American citizens, you have unjustly imprisoned. Protect foreign journalists, diplomats and aid workers in your country. Close immediately and permanently every terrorist training camp in Afghanistan, and hand over every terrorist, and every person in their support structure, to appropriate authorities. Give the United States full access to terrorist training camps, so we can make sure they are no longer operating .

"These demands are not open to negotiation or discussion. The Taliban must act, and act immediately. They will hand over the terrorists, or they will share in their fate."

– President George W. Bush, 20 September 2001 address to a joint session of Congress.

and Ramzi Yousef in Manila, the Philippines in 1995. A computer seized from Murad contained details of a plot to hijack an airliner and crash it into CIA Headquarters in Langley, Virginia. Murad confessed that he had attended several US flight schools while obtaining a commercial pilot license. He stated that at least ten other Middle Eastern men had done the same thing. The investigation also pointed to a Muslim cleric who has been implicated in the 11 September attacks. The Filipino police shared this information with the US Federal Bureau of Investigation (FBI).

Like so many 'surprise attacks,' the 11 September assaults were not a

On the day before his joint address to Congress, President Bush had ordered US military aircraft to Persian Gulf bases. He also ordered

Armorers use a lift truck to load 2000 pound (907.2 KG) Joint Direct Attack Munition (JDAM) bombs onto a B-52H. US and British forces attacked 31 targets on the first night of the war on terror. Warships launched 50 Tomahawk cruise missiles at Afghanistan. In a telling indictment of the Taliban air defense system, B-52s flew in those initial attacks, despite their large radar cross-section. B-52s were deployed from the 5th Bomb Wing at Minot Air Force Base (AFB), North Dakota and the 917th Wing (Wg) from Barksdale AFB, Louisiana. (USAF)

The initial attacks on the terrorist infrastructure began at 2045 hours local (Afghan) time on 7 October 2001. B-52s were in the vanguard of these attacks. The 'Buff' (Big Ugly Fat Fellow) is the oldest aircraft in the US inventory, having celebrated the 50th anniversary of its first flight on 15 April 2002. The NYPD on the nose – with 11 SEPT 01 above it and WE REMEMBER below – recalled the New York Police Department (NYPD) personnel killed at the World Trade Center. (USAF by SSgt Larry A. Simmons)

Navy carrier battle groups to the Indian Ocean to prepare for an attack on Taliban and al-Qaeda forces in Afghanistan. The President informed Congress of the impending attacks on 6 October.

The first strikes of Operation ENDURING FREEDOM were launched at 1630 hours Coordinated Universal Time[4] (1230 hours EDT) on 7 October 2001. Multi-pronged and multi-national attacks were made against Afghanistan's Taliban regime and the al-Qaeda organization of Osama bin Laden. British and US submarines and ships launched more than 50 **BGM-109 Tomahawk** cruise missiles against terrorist training camps and Taliban infrastructure. Air strikes were flown by **B-1 Lancer**, **B-2 Spirit**, and **B-52 Stratofortress** heavy bombers. Tactical aircraft from US carrier groups in the Indian Ocean also flew missions against the most readily identifiable targets. Simultaneously, food supplies were dropped to Afghan refugees by high-flying **C-17 Globemaster III** transports.

The air campaign initially focused on Taliban and al-Qaeda infrastructure. There was little infrastructure to attack and American Special Forces were inserted into Afghanistan within a few weeks. The Special Forces accompanied a variety of Afghan groups who were intent on driving the Taliban from power. Most of these groups were made up of diverse tribal groups who owed their primary allegiance to local warlords or tribal leaders. Foremost of these anti-Taliban groups is the Northern Alliance, also called the United Front. The US-led coalition of Great Britain, France, Australia, Canada, the Czech Republic, Germany, Italy, New Zealand, Poland, Russia, and Turkey kept these groups focused on the rapidly advancing military campaign.

The Taliban had been driven from effective power when the Northern Alliance entered Kabul on 14 November. The remnants of the government and al-Qaeda troops had fled south towards Kandahar. The Marines landed there to cut off the Taliban from their last stronghold. They were now forced into caves in eastern Afghanistan, in the Tora Bora Mountains and Paktia Province. A protracted campaign ensued to search out and destroy the remnants of al-Qaeda.

[4] Coordinated Universal Time (UTC) is also called Greenwich Mean Time (GMT) in some countries.

JDAMs are loaded onto the port wing pylon of a B-52H prior to an ENDURING FREEDOM mission. Attacks on Taliban and al-Qaeda terrorist training camps and associated facilities continued around the clock. The B-52s came from a variety of squadrons and were integrated into the 28th Expeditionary Wing, based on the Indian Ocean atoll of Diego Garcia. They carried a variety of bombs, including the 2000 pound JDAM, a conventional bomb with Global Positioning System (GPS) and inertial guidance units added to the tail section to enhance precision guidance. (USAF by SSgt Larry A. Simmons)

GARMABAK GHAR TERRORIST TRAINING CAMP, AFGHANISTAN
POST STRIKE

(Above) Afghanistan had only 13 airfields at the beginning of the war, and approximately eight of the Taliban's 40 combat aircraft were flyable. Nevertheless, the coalition ensured early air supremacy by knocking out Taliban airfields. Shindad Airfield's runway and taxiways were cratered in one of the initial raids. This post-strike image recorded the precision of these attacks. Photo interpreters added arrows to indicate bomb hits on runways and taxiways. (USAF)

(Above left and left) The devastation of the Garmabak Ghar terrorist training camp is displayed in these before and after photos taken by a US reconnaissance aircraft. This camp was one of 31 targets struck on the first night of Operation ENDURING FREEDOM. (USAF)

A B-52H Stratofortress flies en route to Diego Garcia after a strike against Taliban and al-Qaeda installations. Boeing built 102 B-52Hs in 1960-61, of which 85 remain on active duty and nine in the Air Force Reserve. Eight 17,000 pound thrust Pratt & Whitney TF-33 turbofan engines power the B-52H to a maximum speed of 595 MPH (957.5 KMH). Weapons pylons are mounted on the inboard wing undersurfaces, while 700 gallon (2649.8 L) fuel tanks are placed on the outboard wings. The B-52H's maximum takeoff weight is 505,000 pounds (229,068 KG). This weight includes a maximum ordnance load of 50,000 pounds (22,680 KG). (USAF by TSgt Cedric H. Rudisill)

The B-52H's wing pylons each hold six 2000 pound JDAMs. Because JDAM is targeted using latitude/longitude coordinates, targets do not have to be acquired visually. JDAMs can be launched up to 15 miles (24.1 KM) from a target, depending upon the launch aircraft's speed and altitude. (USAF)

A refueler adjusts the fuel hose supplying a 917th Wg B-52H on Diego Garcia. This atoll is a British possession located 7° south of the Equator in the Indian Ocean. It comprises 6720 acres (2719.6 hectares) with 40 miles (64.4 KM) of shoreline. Diego Garcia's shoreline encloses a lagoon 6.5 miles (10.5 KM) wide and 13 miles (20.9 KM) long. The US began constructing a Naval Communications Facility on the atoll in 1971, followed by other military installations. B-52s extensively used Diego Garcia's air base for Operation DESERT STORM against Iraq in 1991. B-52s, B-1s, and B-2s operated from this base for ENDURING FREEDOM. (USAF)

(Right) Armorers load 500 pound (226.8 KG) Mk 82 'iron' bombs into a B-52H's weapons bay for a trip to Afghanistan. The Stratofortress can internally carry 27 Mk 82 or 750 pound (340.2 KG) Mk 117 bombs. Additional weapons can be mounted on the two wing pylons. (USAF)

Ground crewmen load 2000 pound JDAMs into a Northrop Grumman B-2 Spirit in its hangar at Whiteman AFB, Missouri. The 'Stealth Bomber' flew its missions from Whiteman, home of the 509th BW. B-2s were employed to deliver the new 4700 pound (2131.9 KG) GBU-37 'bunker buster' deep penetrating bomb against al-Qaeda cave complexes. The GBU-37 is guided by both Global Positioning System (GPS) satellites and by the aircraft's Inertial Guidance System (INS). (USAF)

7

A B-2A taxies to parking on Diego Garcia after a 30+ hour mission to bomb Taliban positions in Afghanistan. A relief crew stood by to fly the Spirit back to Whiteman AFB. Six B-2s participated in the first three days of ENDURING FREEDOM. Engines were not shut down during crew changes at Diego Garcia. The 70 straight hours of running highlighted the reliability of the four 19,000 pound thrust General Electric GE-F118-GE-110 engines. (USAF by SRA Rebeca M. Luquin)

A B-2A drops a 2000 pound JDAM during testing. High open/close speed bomb bay doors minimize the exposure time of the relatively high radar signature the open doors present. B-2 strikes on 9 October utilized the 4700 pound GBU-37 for the first time. This deep penetrating bomb has a Circular Error Probable (CEP) of 12 to 18 M (39.4 to 59.1 feet). CEP is the radius of a circle at the desired point of impact, which contains half of the bombs independently aimed to hit this point. The GBU-37 has a unit cost of $231,250. (USAF)

(Below) A KC-135 Stratotanker refuels a B-2A en route to its target in Afghanistan. The Spirit's unrefueled range is approximately 6000 miles (9655.8 KM). Missions to Afghanistan exceeded 8000 miles (12,874.4 KM) between Whiteman AFB and Diego Garcia, which required several in-flight refuelings during the mission. (USAF)

(Above) The B-2 is the newest and – at $1.3 billion each – most expensive US bomber to see combat. Northrop Grumman built 22 Spirits, with 16 of these assigned to the 509th BW. The B-2A can carry up to 50,000 pounds (22,680 KG) of ordnance. Its crew of two pilots relieve each other during the long missions. (USAF)

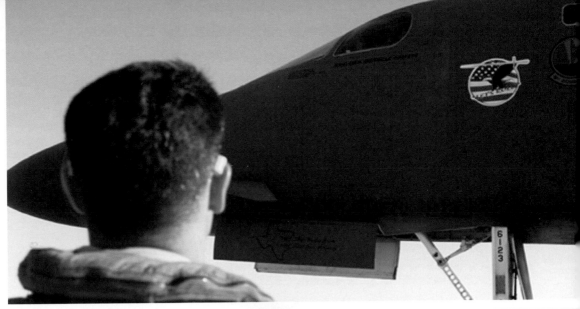

The "LET'S ROLL!" artwork on this 9th Bomb Squadron B-1B (86-0126) reflects one of the more inspirational expressions to emerge from America's war on terror. Todd Beamer, a passenger on United Airlines Flight 93, made this his call to action to fellow passengers before fighting the terrorists who had hijacked the Boeing 757 on 11 September 2001. "Let's Roll!" became a call to arms for the entire nation. (USAF by TSgt Malin G. Zimmerman)

A USAF ordnance specialist gives directions for loading a 2000 pound JDAM on a Rockwell B-1B Lancer on Diego Garcia. JDAMs were first used in combat over Kosovo (Operation ALLIED FORCE) in 1999. A tail assembly incorporating GPS/INS navigation sensors is added to a 'dumb' bomb to create a 'super-smart' JDAM. B-1s can carry 24 JDAMs, eight in each of the three bomb bays. (USAF by SSgt Shane Cuomo)

(Right) A B-1B crew confers with their crew chief prior to an ENDURING FREEDOM mission. The 'Bone' crew consists of Pilot, Co-Pilot, Offensive Systems Operator (OSO), and Defensive Systems Operator (DSO). Both the OSO and DSO are cross-trained to perform each other's duties during a mission. (USAF by SSgt Shane Cuomo)

(Below) A B-1B in full afterburner departs Diego Garcia for Afghanistan. Bomber missions from Diego Garcia were often 12-15 hours in length, covering up to 5500 miles (8851.2 KM). In the first three weeks of the campaign, the 28th Expeditionary Wing (EW) delivered 80% of all bombs dropped on Afghanistan. A B-1 from Ellsworth was the first fixed-wing loss of the war, going down in the Indian Ocean 60 miles (96.6 KM) north of Diego Garcia. The four-man crew was later rescued by the destroyer USS RUSSELL (DDG-59). (USAF)

Crew chiefs stand by while flight crews prepare to start engines for another B-1 mission against Taliban and al-Qaeda positions in Afghanistan. The B-1 has an empty weight of 192,000 pounds (87,091.2 KG) and can carry 195,000 pounds (88,452 KG) of internal fuel. It has a gross takeoff weight of 477,000 pounds (216,367.2 KG) and can carry up to 75,000 pounds (34,020 KG) of ordnance in three bomb bays. (USAF)

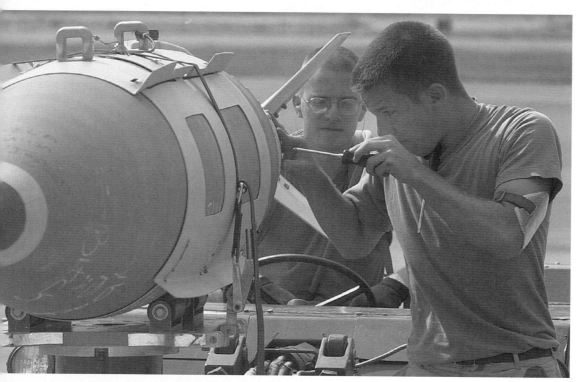

A weapons technician makes final adjustments before loading a JDAM on a B-1B. The JDAM packages are contained in the tail assembly of standard Mk 80 series bombs. Their unit cost is approximately $20,000 and they are capable of hitting within 40 feet (12.2 M) of their targets in all weather. Laser-guided bombs, which cost $100,000 each, are hindered by bad weather conditions. An umbilical connecting the aircraft's system to the JDAM updates the weapon's GPS and inertial systems in real time, until release. While laser-guided GBUs were the stars of the Gulf War, JDAMS are the stars of ENDURING FREEDOM. Three of the four tail section fins are moveable to provide steering commands during the bomb's free-fall. (USAF)

A load of 2000 pound GBU-36/B JDAMs is readied for loading on a B-1B at Diego Garcia. The Lancer missions' airborne portion lasted 15 hours, while the total mission planning, briefing, and debriefing times were 24 hours. The B-1s dropped more munitions on Afghanistan than any other single aircraft type. (USAF by SSgt Shane Cuomo)

An Air Force weapons loader from the 28th Air Expeditionary Wing (AEW) loads a 2000 pound JDAM on a B-1B. By 20 November 2001, over 10,000 bombs were dropped on Afghanistan – 60% of which were precision-guided munitions. The Wing's eight B-1s were flying four sorties per day, each averaging 15 hours. (USAF photo by SSgt Larry A. Simmons)

B-1 ground crewmen take a break by an access ladder during around-the-clock operations. Early in the campaign, they had virtually no time off as they worked to maintain and load the 'Bones.' The crew entry steps just behind the nose gear display wear from the constant use in ENDURING FREEDOM missions. (USAF)

(Below) An unlikely star of the war on terrorism is the General Atomics Predator Unmanned Aerial Vehicle (UAV). The Predator is a Joint Forces Air Commander-owned theater asset for reconnaissance, surveillance, and target acquisition in support of the Joint Forces commander. It has a wingspan of 47 feet (14.3 M), a maximum gross weight of 2100 pounds (952.6 KG), and a range of 500 miles (804.7 KM), with 24 hours on station. Predators operate in 'teams' of four aircraft. They were among the first assets requested by Central Command (CENTCOM) Commander General Tommy Franks.

(Above) The 15,000 pound (6804 KG) BLU-82B 'Daisy Cutter' is the largest conventional munition in existence. It is delivered by an MC-130 via parachute extraction from the cargo compartment. Originally designed to clear jungles to create landing zones in Vietnam, the 'Daisy Cutter' was used as an anti-personnel weapon in Afghanistan. The BLU-82B's lethal radius ranges from 300 to 900 feet (91.4 to 274.3 M), depending upon the terrain. (USAF)

Predators were used to launch AGM-114 Hellfire missiles to attack highly mobile al-Qaeda forces. They have provided real-time targeting information to precision munitions equipped strike aircraft. (USAF by TSgt Scott Reed)

11

Lt Col James Horton, Commander of the 79th FS, 20th FW from Shaw AFB, South Carolina flies an F-16CJ Fighting Falcon over western Colorado. This flight occurred during a large force employment exercise, held in conjunction with the Inaugural Tiger Meet of the Americas in the fall of 2001. The meet was held simultaneously with Operation NOBLE EAGLE, the Barrier Combat Air Patrol (BARCAP) of the Continental United States (CONUS) following the 11 September attacks. This F-16CJ is armed with AIM-9 Sidewinder missiles under the wings and AIM-120 Advanced Medium-Range Air-to-Air Missiles (AAMRAMs) on the wingtips. NOBLE EAGLE BARCAPs were flown by regular Air Force, Air Force Reserve Command (AFRC), and Air National Guard (ANG) units. (USAF by SSgt Greg L. Davis)

An F-16 of the 177th FW, New Jersey Air National Guard (ANG), flies a CAP mission past Atlantic City, New Jersey. This was flown in support of Operation NOBLE EAGLE, the program of 24 hour CAPs flown by ANG and Reserve Squadrons. These patrols were flown over much of the homeland to guard against further terrorist attacks. (USAF by MSgt Don Taggart)

An F-15C Eagle from the 27th FS, 1st FW at Langley AFB, Virginia, overflies Washington, DC during an early morning combat air patrol mission in support of Operation NOBLE EAGLE. The Pentagon with its damaged west side lies under the Eagle's starboard wing. Air Supremacy over Afghanistan meant the ability to fly anywhere, anytime without being challenged by enemy anti-air. Ironically, all the anti-air combat air patrols during ENDURING FREEDOM were flown over the CONUS. (USAF by SSgt Greg L. Davis)

While ENDURING FREEDOM monopolized the media and the public's attention, Operation SOUTHERN WATCH continued to patrol the southern no fly zone of Iraq – another focus of the war on terror. An F-16 pilot of the 523rd FS, 27th FW from Cannon AFB, New Mexico sends a Valentine's Day message to people back home. (USAF by TSgt Jack Braden)

The Boeing/Grumman E-8 Joint Surveillance Target Attack Radar System (J-STARS) is a modified Boeing 707-320B airliner with a ventral radar. This allows the E-8 to scan the ground up to 150 miles (241.4 км) away with a 120° field of view. It is used to track and assign ground targets to strike aircraft. The 93rd Control Wing at Tinker AFB, Oklahoma operates J-STARS, which deploy in support of US operations worldwide. (USAF)

(Right) The nose art on this Boeing KC-135E Stratotanker (57-1464) says it all: The KC-135 has been in USAF service since 1957. Boeing produced 732 KC-135s between 1956 and 1965 and nearly 500 of these remain in service with USAF, ANG, and Air Force Reserve Command (AFRC) units. The Stratotankers were modified with more powerful and fuel-efficient engines, along with reskinned lower wing surfaces to increase service life. The latest KC-135Rs can carry 209,289 pounds (94,933.5 кg) of fuel. (USAF)

(Below) The Boeing E-3 Sentry Airborne Warning And Control System (AWACS) is a modified Boeing 707-320B with a 30 foot (9.1 м) diameter rotating radar dome 14 feet (4.3 м) above the rear fuselage. AWACS is used to keep track of airborne traffic. It was used extensively over CONUS in the days following the 11 September attacks. This effort included 17 E-3s of the North Atlantic Treaty Organization (NATO) Airborne Early Warning Force, which deployed from their home base at Geilenkirchen, Germany. (USAF)

13

A McDonnell Douglas F-15E Strike Eagle stands ready for a night mission against Taliban and al-Qaeda forces. F-15Es of the 391st FS, 366th Air Expeditionary Wing (AEW) were deployed to Central Asian airbases for Operation ENDURING FREEDOM. It is believed that the Eagles flew from Kyrgyzstan and/or Tajikistan – both former Soviet republics – for strikes against neighboring Afghanistan. Missions were flown around the clock, using the F-15E's sophisticated targeting pods. (USAF by MSgt Dave Nolan)

An Air Force crew chief from the 332nd Air Expeditionary Group (AEG) checks one of the F-15Es prior to the crew's arrival. He stands on the crew access ladder used to enter and exit the cockpit. Strike Eagles have a gross takeoff weight of 81,000 pounds (36,741.6 KG), compared to 68,000 pounds (30,844.8 KG) for the F-15C air superiority fighter. This weight increase is due to the heavier air-to-ground weapons carried by this variant. (USAF by MSgt Dave Nolan)

A Strike Eagle pilot performs a pre-flight walk around prior to an attack mission. Two 23,450 pound Pratt & Whitney F-100-PW-220 afterburning turbofan engines power this Eagle variant. The F-15E is a two seat, two engine dual role fighter capable of speeds up to Mach 2.5 (1650 MPH/2655.3 KMH). It performs day and night all weather air-to-air and air-to-ground missions including strategic strike, interdiction, and Close Air Support (CAS) missions. (USAF by MSgt Dave Nolan)

An F-15E pilot checks with the ground crew before taxiing for takeoff. His ACES II ejection seat is used by many USAF combat aircraft, including the F-16, A-10, B-1, and B-2. Strike Eagles flew their first missions over Afghanistan on 17 October 2001. Operating from airbases in Central Asia reduced the F-15E's mission times, which allowed more strike missions to be flown. These bases were built and used by the Soviet Air Force prior to the Soviet Union's collapse in December of 1991. (USAF)

Crew chiefs from the 332nd AEG prepare to launch an F-15E Strike Eagle on a joint strike mission on 19 November 2001. The Strike Eagles departed from their operating location north of Afghanistan in support of Coalition forces. The F-15Es were among 65 strike aircraft that flew against Taliban and al-Qaeda forces. Two thirds of this force came from carriers in the Indian Ocean. (USAF by MSgt Dave Nolan)

Nose art on 332nd AEG F-15Es had a consistent theme. NEVER FORGET is the war on terror's equivalent of 'Remember Pearl Harbor' during World War Two. Laser Guided Bomb (LGB) silhouettes served as mission markers. The wedge missing from the Pentagon indicated one of the terrorist strikes, while the use of the Twin Towers from the New York skyline was an imaginative way to represent 9-11-01. (Via John Gourley)

An Air Force crew chief checks a LGB on a 332nd AEW F-15E prior to a strike mission. An AIM-9 Sidewinder Air-to-Air Missile (AAM) is mounted on the pylon's side. The F-15E can carry up to 24,250 pounds (10,999.8 KG) of ordnance on external hard points. These weapons include unguided and guided air-to-surface munitions and AAMs for self-defense. The Strike Eagle is crewed by a pilot and a Weapons System Operator (WSO). (USAF by MSgt Dave Nolan)

The New York Police Department (NYPD) insignia is placed on the nose of this 332nd AEG F-15E. Covers were placed over the pitot tube on the lower nose and the Angle Of Attack (AOA) sensor high on the nose side. The red REMOVE BEFORE FLIGHT streamer attached to the AOA cover is a reminder for ground crew. (Via John Gourley)

A tiger is painted on the nose of this 332nd AEW F-15E, above the Twin Towers artwork. A large number of mission tallies – represented by LGB silhouettes – appears aft of the nose art. The eagle's head above the mission markers is part of the crew name box. (Via John Gourley)

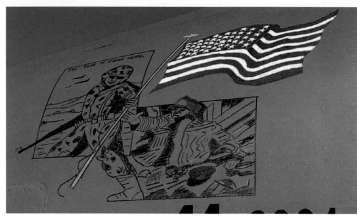

The nose art on this F-15E features a US soldier taking a US flag from a New York fire fighter in the rubble. The soldier says, "We'll take it from here," the phrase written above the soldier's head. (Via John Gourley)

The Fire Department of New York (FDNY) insignia is painted on this F-15E's nose, in tribute to the fire fighters killed at the World Trade Center on 11 September 2001. Bomb silhouettes for 35 missions are painted aft of the FDNY badge. (Via John Gourley)

Mountain Home Eagles stand on the ramp at their 'Forward Deployed Base,' prior to continuing strikes on terrorist cells. In a telling statement, General Tommy Franks said that the 200 sorties flown per day in Operation ENDURING FREEDOM were hitting roughly the same number of targets that 3000 sorties per day hit in DESERT STORM. This quantum leap in accuracy was achieved in just ten years of munitions development. (USAF by MSgt Dave Nolan)

Two AGM-130As are placed on a weapons trailer near a waiting F-15E. The AGM-130A is one of the newest precision munitions in the US arsenal. It is essentially a GBU-15 LGB with an attached rocket motor, giving it a range of 40 miles (64.4 KM). It carries GPS/INS guidance units, along with a Television/Infra-Red (TV/IR) terminal guidance unit. The launch weight of 2917 pounds (1323.2 KG) includes a 2000 pound (907.2 KG) warhead. The F-15E can carry two of these missiles, one under each wing. Each AGM-130A costs $884,279! (USAF)

(Above) 'Pugs,' an F-15E WSO, does a pre-flight walk around prior to the first Strike Eagle missions in Operation ENDURING FREEDOM. Some 332nd AEW members honored the FDNY by wearing its patch on the flight suit's right sleeve, instead of the US flag normally worn there. This Strike Eagle is armed with Laser Guided Bombs (LGBs) for attacking terrorist positions and – in the unlikely event of an airborne threat – AIM-9 and AIM-120 missiles. (USAF by MSgt Dave Nolan)

(Right) A ground crew sends off a Strike Eagle as it departs on the war's first F-15E attack mission. The AN/AAQ-13 Low-Altitude Navigation and Targeting Infrared for Night (LANTIRN) navigation pod is mounted under the starboard engine intake. This pod contains a Forward Looking Infra-Red (FLIR) sensor above a terrain following radar. The FLIR image is displayed on the pilot's Heads-Up Display (HUD), allowing low level navigation at night. (USAF)

(Below) A crew chief stands by during an F-15E's engine start procedure. Bombs are mounted on pylons attached to low-drag Conformal Fuel Tanks (CFTs) fitted to the fuselage sides. The CFTs provide an additional 1500 gallons (5678.1 L) of fuel. Although these tanks slightly degrade performance, they are a much better alternative than external (wing) tanks. CFTs sufficiently extend the F-15E's range to allow all other external stores stations to be used for weapons. (USAF by MSgt Dave Nolan)

(Above) A Boeing C-17A Globemaster III lands at Ramstein Air Base (AB), Germany after a mission over Afghanistan. The C-17 is the newest airlifter to enter the Air Force inventory, with its first flight in 1991. The C-17 is the third Air Force cargo aircraft to be dubbed 'Globemaster,' after the earlier Douglas C-74 and C-124. It has an unrefueled range of 5200 nautical miles (5987.9 statute miles/9636.3 KM) at a cruise speed of 450 knots (518.2 MPH/833.9 KMH). (USAF)

(Left) Five C-17s are lined up at Ramstein AB between missions. In the war's first month, 78 C-17s transited the Ukrainian corridor over the Black Sea en route to Afghanistan. During December of 2001, C-17s made nightly visits to Forward Operating Base (FOB) Rhino, near Kandahar, Afghanistan. They flew 43 missions into Rhino, delivering 1450 tons (1315.4 MT) of heavy equipment and 419 passengers. Humanitarian sorties had grown to 162, with 2.5 million individual rations dropped. (USAF)

(Left) A C-17A (96-0006) of the 437th Airlift Wing (AW) is loaded with Tri-Wall Aerial Delivery (TRIAD) containers full of humanitarian daily rations. The wing deployed from its home of Charleston AFB, South Carolina to Ramstein AB for ENDURING FREEDOM. Globemaster IIIs flew humanitarian missions to drop rations to the starving population of the Taliban-controlled country. These missions occurred parallel to US air strikes against the terrorists. (USAF by MSgt John P. Snow)

(Below) Loadmasters aboard a C-17 prepare to drop humanitarian daily rations over Afghanistan in this IR image. Air Force loadmasters Senior MSgt Cliff Harmon and MSgt Donny Brass developed the method for air dropping rations from high altitude without parachutes. They use special cardboard boxes, which measure 40 inches (101.6 CM) by 48 inches (121.9 CM) by 84 inches (213.4 CM). The C-17's navigation system allows air drops from high altitude without endangering refugees on the ground. The loadmasters said, "We know exactly where these items are going to land." During the first four nights of the war, C-17s dropped 140,000 individual meals. (USAF)

(Above) A C-17A (99-0061) makes the turn at the end of the runway at Kandahar. It is assigned to the 62nd AW from McCord AFB, Washington. The C-17 can carry up to 170,000 pounds (77,112 KG) of cargo and has a maximum takeoff weight of 585,000 pounds (265,356 KG). It has a crew of three: Pilot, Co-Pilot, and Loadmaster. The US Air Force plans to acquire 120 C-17s, with the last aircraft scheduled for delivery in 2004. Four 40,900 pound thrust Pratt & Whitney F117-PW-100 turbofan engines power the C-17. (USAF)

(Right) Loadmasters and ground crew load a camouflaged metal container aboard a C-17A (97-0047) prior to an ENDURING FREE-DOM mission. This container is believed to be used for temporary equipment storage or office space for forward deployed units. Another Globemaster III is parked in the background. (USAF)

(Right) A Lockheed C-5 Galaxy approaches a KC-135 for an aerial refueling during Operation ENDURING FREEDOM. The first operational C-5s were delivered to the 437th Military Airlift Wing, Charleston AFB, South Carolina in June of 1970. The Galaxy has a maximum takeoff weight of 840,000 pounds (381,024 KG), and can carry 204,000 pounds (92,534.4 KG) of cargo. (USAF)

(Below) Two C-5s are lined up at a US air base, while a C-17 is parked at the end of the line. The Galaxy will continue to be an important aspect of the USAF world-wide mobility commitment, especially with the retirement of the even older Lockheed C-141 Starlifter. This importance comes despite the C-5 having the highest operating cost of any USAF weapon system. USAF, ANG, and Reserve airlift squadrons operate 109 C-5s. (USAF)

19

(Above) The Lockheed C-130 Hercules is the world's most widely used airlifter, serving with over 60 different countries. It has been in production since 1956 and continues to provide combat airlift into forward operating locations in Operation ENDURING FREEDOM. Army troops load a C-130H of the 37th AS at Ramstein AB, Germany, headed for Afghanistan. The Squadron is assigned to the 435th AW from Rhein Main AB, Germany. (USAF by MSgt Keith Reed)

(Left) Airmen from the 16th Special Operations Wing (SOW) at Hurlburt Field, Florida unload one of their Sikorsky MH-53J PAVE LOW III helicopters from a C-17A at Kandahar. US Special Forces were among the first American ground troops in the war, acting as advisors and coordinating the heavy aerial bombardment of the Taliban. (USAF by TSgt Scott Reed)

Major Jeffery Dunn (left) and 1Lt Joseph Mondello run through the pre-take off checklist aboard their McDonnell Douglas C-9A Nightingale. The crew — assigned to the 75th AS, 86th AW at Ramstein AB, Germany — were preparing to depart from Izmir Air Station, Turkey. The pilots flew a medical team throughout the European Theatre to pick up and deliver patients. The C-9A is a military medical evacuation version of the DC-9 airliner. (USAF by MSgt Keith Reed)

(Above) The crew of a USAF C-130 makes the final turn on approach to Kandahar, Afghanistan during Operation ENDURING FREEDOM. This cargo version of the Hercules has the straightforward instrument panel. C-130 gunship and special operations variants have a variety of sophisticated navigation and attack sensors and displays in the cockpit. These pilots wear the tan flight suits authorized for Southwest Asia, instead of the USAF's standard olive green suits. (USAF)

(Right) An Air Force engine technician performs maintenance on a T-56-A-15 engine of a C-130H (74-1679). This Hercules was one of the airlifters deployed to the Afghanistan theatre for Operation ENDURING FREEDOM. Four 4910 shaft horsepower (SHP) Allison T-56-A-15 turboprop engines power this Hercules variant. The YC-130 prototype of 1954 used four 3250 SHP YT-56A-1s. The first C-130A Hercules entered USAF service in December of 1955. Today, over 60 countries operate C-130s. (USAF)

Captain John Meier, a C-130 Hercules pilot from Aviano AB, Italy, heads towards a 'forward-deployed' base in Afghanistan on 22 February 2002. The yellow wheel over his left shoulder is used for nose-wheel steering. This allows the C-130 pilot to steer the aircraft's nose landing gear during ground taxiing, complementing the use of differential engine throttling. (USAF by MSgt Keith Reed)

21

The EC-130E COMMANDO SOLO II was an early and important player in the war against the Taliban. While Coalition bombers pounded the Taliban and al-Qaeda into submission, COMMANDO SOLO aircraft broadcast news, information, and music to the Afghan population. These people had virtually no information and entertainment during the Taliban's five-year rule. Television and radio antennas are mounted on the EC-130E's vertical tail. The 193rd Special Operations Squadron, 193rd Special Operations Wing of the Pennsylvania ANG flies EC-130Es. The unit is based at Harrisburg International Airport (IAP), Pennsylvania. (USAF)

An MC-130H COMBAT TALON II refuels at night from a KC-135R tanker out of Burgas, Bulgaria. The MC-130H conducts infiltrations of special operations forces and equipment. These missions are conducted in adverse weather at low-level and long range. Each $72.5 million MC-130H is equipped with the most sophisticated navigation equipment. (USAF by MSgt Blake R. Borsic)

Ground crewmen offload supplies from a C-130 Hercules at Kandahar IAP, Afghanistan on 7 February 2002. The pallet is placed onto a ground loading vehicle, which will carry it from the aircraft. The C-130 can carry up to 43,400 pounds (19,686.2 KG) of cargo to a range of 1428 miles (2298.1 KM). The aircraft is assigned to the 40th AS, 7th Wing at Dyess AFB, Texas. (DOD by PH2 David C. Mercil)

A USAF HC-130P refuels an US Marine Corps (USMC) CH-53E Super Stallion on a special operations mission. The helicopter's nose-mounted refueling probe enters a drogue extended from the HC-130P's wing pod to draw fuel. This allows the helicopter to extend its range for deep penetration special operations. The HC-130P is assigned to the 347th Wing at Moody AFB, Georgia. (USAF)

A KC-135R refuels an AC-130H Spectre gunship en route to Afghanistan. The AC-130 is one of the most effective, if unheralded, combat aircraft in the Air Force inventory. The Spectre's primary missions are close air support, air interdiction and armed reconnaissance. Other missions include perimeter and point defense, escort, landing, drop and extraction zone support, forward air control, limited command and control, and combat search and rescue. The AC-130 first saw action in Vietnam, where it was credited with destroying over 10,000 trucks on the Ho Chi Minh Trail. (USAF)

An AC-130H (69-6569) flies behind another aircraft in the Afghanistan theatre. This Spectre variant is armed with two 20mm M61 cannon, two 40mm Bofors L-60 cannon, and a 105mm M102 howitzer. The later AC-130U replaces the 20mm cannon with one 25mm GAU-12 cannon. Spectres were extensively used to support US-led attacks on Taliban and al-Qaeda positions. (USAF)

The Sikorsky MH-60G PAVE HAWK is operated by the Air Force Special Operations Command (AFSOC), a component of the US Special Operations Command (USSOCOM). The MH-60G's primary wartime missions are infiltration, exfiltration and resupply of special operations forces in day, night or marginal weather conditions. (USAF)

An MH-53J PAVE LOW III flies astern of an HC-130 refueling aircraft. This helicopter is used to infiltrate special forces. It has a top speed of 160 MPH (257.5 KMH) and an unrefueled range of 600 miles (965.6 KM). The MH-53J is armor plated and carries three 7.62MM Miniguns for self-defense. Its navigation system features real-time downloads of information from military satellites, allowing it to penetrate deep behind enemy lines. (USAF)

23

MSgt Bart Decker, an AFSOC combat controller from Hurlburt Field, Florida, accompanied the Northern Alliance on their drive to overthrow the Taliban. He rides a horse to get around the mountainous country, while a colleague is on another horse. Combat controllers provided air traffic control for aircraft supporting Operation ENDURING FREEDOM. They use radios to inform pilots of the location and status of ground targets and assist in Search and Rescue (SAR) of downed aircrew. (USAF)

A US Navy SEAL (SEa-Air-Land) conducts a special reconnaissance on a suspected al-Qaeda and Taliban position on 24 January 2002. Aircraft infiltrated him and his colleagues from warships in the Arabian Sea into Afghanistan. SEALs worked in conjunction with other US Special Forces. These forces spotted targets for US aircraft, aided in recovering downed aircrews, and worked with Northern Alliance forces in opposing the Taliban. (US Navy by PH1 (AW) Tim Turner)

(Left) One of the first offensive operations executed by US Special Forces was a night parachute drop on a Taliban barracks. These troops used a highly maneuverable parachute canopy, which had windows cut into the skirt and gores to provide forward motion. Pulling on steering lines attached to the aft risers provided directional control by closing these windows. (USAF)

(Below) PFC Michael Williams (left) spots sniping targets for SSgt Kevin Lacrosse during an operation near Bagram, Afghanistan. The soldiers are assigned to the Headquarters and Headquarters Company, 1st Battalion, 87th Infantry Regiment, 10th Mountain Division. The Division deployed from its home of Fort Drum, New York. (US Army by SSgt Jon D. Sheffer)

A Boeing (formerly McDonnell Douglas) AH-64A Apache leaves a Forward Operating Location (FOL) for a Close Air Support (CAS) mission in Afghanistan. The AH-64 provided effective CAS during Operation ANACONDA, the campaign against al-Qaeda strongholds in southern Afghanistan in March of 2002. The Apache has a standard day ceiling of 21,000 feet (6400.8 M), which was crucial during ANACONDA battles in the Afghan mountains. The AH-64A's maximum speed is 184 MPH (296.1 KMH) and its range is 260 miles (418.4 KM). Its two-man crew consists of a co-pilot/gunner in the front seat and a pilot in the back seat. (US Army)

(Right) A technician services an AH-64A Apache parked on Pierced Steel Planking (PSP) at a FOL in Afghanistan. The AH-64 is the US Army's principal attack helicopter, after winning a 1973-76 competition to replace the AH-1 Cobra. The Apache is transportable in both C-5 and C-17 aircraft. It has an outstanding combat record, beginning in Panama and continuing in Operation DESERT STORM, where it opened the war by destroying Iraqi early warning radars with AGM-114 Hellfire missiles. Its stub wings carry four articulating weapons pylons. This Apache has 2.75 inch (70MM) folding-fin rocket pods on outboard stations, an external fuel tank, and Hellfire missile launch rails on the inboard stations. A 30MM M230 chain gun is mounted under the nose. (US Army)

Northern Alliance soldiers stand on their gun truck before engaging Taliban forces. This vehicle – believed to be a Soviet-built Ural 4320 truck – is armed with a 23MM ZU-23/2 twin-barrel anti-aircraft cannon. The ZU-23/2 fires 200 rounds per minute out to 7000 M (22,965.9 feet) against ground targets and 5000 M (16,404.2 feet) against aircraft. A lifetime of war makes for Afghan creativity when developing one-of-kind weapons systems.

A Navy SEAL observes munitions being destroyed on 12 February 2002. SEALs discovered the cache of munitions while conducting a Sensitive Site Exploitation (SSE) mission in eastern Afghanistan. He is carrying the 5.56MM M4 Carbine, equipped with an M68 sight. The M68 is a reflex (non-telescopic) sight, which uses a red aiming reference (collimated dot) and is designated for the 'two eyes open' method of sighting. This method allows for quick acquisition of the target with high hit probability. (US Navy by PH1 Tim Turner)

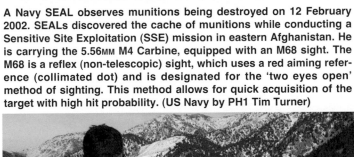

Two US troops stand by a M1109 High Mobility Multi-Purpose Wheeled Vehicle (HMMWV) in Afghanistan. A colleague inside the HMMWV aims the .50 caliber (12.7MM) M2 machine gun at suspected Taliban or al-Qaeda forces. The roof-mounted mount can carry either the 7.62MM M60 machine gun or the 40MM Mk 19 grenade launcher instead of the M2.

Two Northern Alliance T-54/55 series tanks move past mountainous terrain in northern Afghanistan. These Soviet-built vehicles each have a 100MM turret-mounted main gun, with a co-axial 7.62MM machine gun. Both the Northern Alliance and the Taliban used tanks and other armored vehicles left behind by the Soviets when they withdrew from Afghanistan in 1988.

A Boeing MH-47E Chinook flies low during operations in eastern Afghanistan. The MH-47E is the special operations version of the CH-47 Chinook transport helicopter. An in-flight refueling probe is mounted on the MH-47E's starboard nose, while a APQ-174 Terrain Following Radar (TFR) is fitted to the port nose. The slightly extended nose – borrowed from civilian Chinooks – houses weather radar. A Forward Looking Infra-Red (FLIR) turret is mounted under the nose. Enlarged sponsons for additional fuel are fitted along the fuselage sides. It has an unrefueled range of 300 nautical miles (345.5 statute miles/555.9 KM), a service ceiling of 20,000 feet (6096 M), and a payload of over 26,000 pounds (11,793.6 KG). The MH-47E is armed with two 7.62MM Miniguns and a .50 caliber machine gun on the rear ramp. Avionics include AVR-2A laser warning receivers, Global Positioning System (GPS), jammers, chaff and flare dispensers, Night Vision Goggle (NVG), and Satellite Communications (SATCOM) capability.

Special Forces load a MH-47E Chinook in preparation for an attack on al-Qaeda positions in eastern Afghanistan. The basic CH-47 has a maximum takeoff weight of 50,000 pounds (22,680 KG) and a maximum speed of 196 MPH (315.4 KMH). The Chinook can carry up to 38 troops or 24 litters. The CH-47 has been in continuous US Army service since 1962 and is the service's largest and longest-serving helicopter. (US Army)

Soldiers hurry to load ammunition onto a waiting CH-47 Chinook helicopter, which took off to deliver the cargo to troops fighting in the mountains near Gardez, Afghanistan. This scene repeated itself many times as US and Afghan Northern Alliance forces launched a ground offensive against Taliban and al-Qaeda forces. (US Air Force by MSgt Keith Reed)

101st Airborne Division (Air Assault) troopers run for cover after jumping from their MH-47. The Division – based at Fort Campbell, Kentucky – rapidly deploys to trouble spots anywhere in the world. US Special Operations troops, who landed in the midst of the enemy, fought the opening battles in Operation ANACONDA in March of 2002. (US Army)

Three soldiers of the 1st Battalion, 187th Infantry Regiment, 101st Airborne Division (Air Assault) scan the mountains near Gardez, Afghanistan during Operation ANACONDA. Night Vision Goggle (NVG) mounts are clipped to the helmets of two of these troopers. The middle soldier carries radio equipment on his back, including an antenna. US forces in Afghanistan generally wore the three-color desert pattern Battle Dress Uniform (BDU), which entered service in the early 1990s. The Division's 'Screaming Eagle' insignia is worn on the upper left sleeve.

Crouched beside a .50 caliber (12.7MM) Browning M2 machine gun, a soldier peers through his binoculars during Operation ANACONDA. Lens covers hang from straps attached to the front of the binoculars. These covers are placed over the lenses when the binoculars are not in use to protect them from damage. A belt of ammunition runs from an ammunition box on the ground to the machine gun's breech mechanism.

An M2 machine gunner peers through his binoculars at the Afghan countryside. Ground troops in the war against terrorism have advantages not enjoyed by previous generations of American infantrymen. These include special optics, for day and night. They also employ weapons that date to World War Two, including the .50 caliber M2 machine gun. This weapon was originally produced from 1933 until 1946. The M2 was put back into production in 1976 and continues to serve as the primary heavy machine gun for infantry and armor forces.

SEALs search for al-Qaeda and Taliban forces while conducting a Sensitive Site Exploitation mission in the Jaji Mountains on 12 February 2002. The war against terrorism is unlike any foreign war fought by the United States. The enemy does not wear a uniform and does not have any recognizable regular army units. Special Forces are constituted to deal with these exact threats. USSOCOM, headquartered at MacDill AFB, Florida, has units from the Air Force, Navy, and Army. They are flexible in size and mission, with cultural and language capabilities that are suited to a variety of theaters of operations. There are approximately 46,000 troops in USSOCOM. (US Navy by PH1 Tim Turner)

On 11 January 2002, SEALs discovered a large cache of munitions in one of the more than 50 caves explored in the Shawar Kili area. The munitions, caves, and several above ground complexes were destroyed by air strikes called in by the SEALs. Precision-guided 'bunker buster' weapons were used on many of these air raids to neutralize al-Qaeda forces. Special forces carefully checked these caves for booby traps left by al-Qaeda. (US Navy)

A Seabee of US Navy Mobile Naval Construction Battalion 113 is viewed through a night vision scope while he provides perimeter security for an unimproved dirt airstrip in Afghanistan. The Battalion deployed from its home of Gulfport, Mississippi for ENDURING FREEDOM. C-17s of the 437th Airlift Wing from Charleston AFB, South Carolina airlanded the Seabees on the dirt strip in the C-17's first ever such operation. (USAF by TSgt Efrain Gonzalez)

US Marines with the 26th Marine Expeditionary Unit (Special Operations Capable) (MEU SOC) file aboard a Boeing CH-46E Sea Knight on 14 December 2001. The Marines carry their field gear and weapons while they board the helicopter on the deck of the helicopter/dock landing ship USS BATAAN (LHD-5). The 26th MEU (SOC) deployed with BATAAN's Amphibious Ready Group in the Arabian Sea in support of Operation ENDURING FREEDOM. (US Navy by CPH Johnny Bivera)

Marines from the 26th MEU (SOC) ride aboard a CH-46E en route from BATAAN to Afghanistan. Marines are a maritime force, which is expeditionary in nature. The MEU is based on naval vessels and is normally built around a reinforced battalion. It is comprised of 2000 troops and is commanded by a Colonel. MEUs are well-suited to the type of situation presented by Operation ENDURING FREEDOM. They carry all the weapons and support needed to sustain them throughout the campaign. (US Navy by CPH Johnny Bivera)

(Right) A CH-46E lands on unimproved Afghan terrain, with dust kicked up by the rotor blades' wash. Serving since 1964, the CH-46 Sea Knight has a maximum gross takeoff weight of 24,300 pounds (11,022.5 KG) and a maximum speed of 145 knots (167 MPH/268.7 KMH). It has a crew of five (pilot, co-pilot, crew chief, and two gunners) and carries 14 combat-loaded troops into battle. The Marines hope to replace the CH-46 with the Bell/Boeing V-22 Osprey tilt-rotor aircraft. (USMC)

(Below) Marines confer near a CH-46E after landing in Afghanistan. The 26th MEU (SOC) provided perimeter security at Kandahar and the newly established Camp Rhino while the Northern Alliance consolidated its victory over the Taliban in late 2001. (USMC)

A pair of 26th MEU (SOC) LAV-25s lead a raid on a suspected al-Qaeda outpost in Kandahar on 1 January 2002. The General Motors of Canada Light Armored Vehicle (LAV)-25 is an 8 x 8 all-terrain, all-weather vehicle, which is air transportable. The LAV-25-C² (Command and Control) in the foreground features a raised hull roof with communications stations in the troop compartment. Unit commanders use this vehicle to control and communicate with their forces while under full armored protection. The Marines operate 50 LAV-25-C²s. The LAV-25 (MC) pulling up from the left is armed with a turret-mounted 25MM Bushmaster cannon. (USMC by LCpl Nathan E. Eason)

Lance Corporal Reyes from Battalion Landing Team 1/1, Bravo Company, 2nd Platoon provides perimeter security during a Rapid Ground Refueling of two Navy H-60 helicopters on 9 November 2001. Reyes is armed with the 5.56MM M249 Squad Automatic Weapon (SAW), fitted with the AN/PVS-4 Night Vision Sight (NVS). (USAF by TSgt Scott Reed)

A Marine with the 26th MEU (SOC), Battalion Landing Team 3/6 provides small arms support while an advance team conducts a Cordon and Search Raid at a suspected al-Qaeda hideout in Afghanistan's

A Light Armored Reconnaissance scout section leader stands fast as US Marines dismount to check the area after a fire fight at Kandahar International Airport, Afghanistan. The LAV-25 (MC) carries six troops in the aft compartment. It is crewed by three men: driver, commander, and gunner. (USMC by Sgt Thomas Michael Corcoran)

Helmand Province on 1 January 2002. He is armed with a 5.56MM M249 SAW, which is equipped with AN/PVS-4 NVS. (US Navy by CPH Johnny Bivera)

Marines of the 26th MEU (SOC) field-tested the new 7.62MM M14 Designated Marksman Rifle (DMR) around Kandahar. The DMR is a precision grade, semi-automatic rifle, derived from the M14 rifle used by US forces during the 1950s and 1960s. It is equipped with a simple mounting system that accommodates both a day optical sighting scope and the AN/PVS-4 'starlight scope.' The DMR also has other night/low level obscurant target engagement equipment common to, or in development for, the infantry battalion. A combination flash suppressor and silencer is mounted on the DMR's muzzle. (USMC by Sgt Andrew D. Pomykai)

A Bell AH-1W Super Cobra is launched from USS PELELIU (LHA-5) on 13 October 2001, while a second AH-1W flies past the ship. PELELIU was one of several amphibious assault ships with Marine Expeditionary Units (MEUs) embarked for Operation ENDURING FREEDOM. (USMC by LCpl Matthew J. Decker)

AH-1W of Helicopter Medium Squadron One Six Five (HMM-165) takes off from USS BON HOMME RICHARD (LHD-6) to support Marines fighting in Operation ANACONDA in March of 2002. The Squadron was part of the Aviation Combat Element of the 13th MEU,

A deck crewman signals an AH-1W pilot prior to launch. The Super Cobra is powered by a pair of 2082 SHP General Electric T700-GE-401 engines, which gives it a speed of 147 knots (169.3 MPH/272.4 KMH) when combat loaded. It is armed with a turret mounted 20MM cannon with 750 rounds and can carry a variety of ordnance. (USMC)

Special Operations Capable (SOC). The Super Cobra provides close air support to Marine ground units. They were based at Camp Rhino and Kandahar during Operation ENDURING FREEDOM. (USMC by LCpl Daniel Kelly)

(Above) A KC-130 Hercules from Marine Aerial Refuel Transport Squadron Three Five Two (VMGR-352) 'Raiders' offloads cargo at a forward operating base. A KC-130 from VMGR-252 'Heavy Haulers' takes off with Marines from the 26th MEU headed back to Kandahar airport. These Squadrons perform both tactical airlift and aerial refueling missions. VMGR-352 deployed from Marine Corps Air Station (MCAS) El Toro, California, while VMGR-252 came from MCAS Cherry Point, North Carolina. (US Navy by CWO2 William D. Crow)

(Left) A VMGR-352 KC-130R (QB/BuNo 160016) lands at a forward operating location to refuel two Navy H-60 helicopters on 9 November 2001. The H-60s were refueled on the ground before they proceeded with their mission. Refueling pods mounted on the outboard wing undersurfaces allow KC-130s to simultaneously refuel two aircraft. The aircraft can carry up to 31,000 pounds (14,061.6 KG) of fuel. A Marine armed with an M259 SAW helps secure the airfield perimeter against Taliban and al-Qaeda attacks. (USAF by TSgt Scott Reed)

A Marine KC-130 pilot flies low over Afghanistan. The Marines have operated three versions of the KC-130 (KC-130F, KC-130R, and KC-130T) since its introduction in the early 1960s. The KC-130 refuels all Marine Corps aircraft and helicopters equipped with in-flight refueling probes. In the transport role, it can carry 26,913 pounds (12,207.7 KG) of cargo or 64 paratroopers. (USMC)

Marines from the 26th MEU prepare to depart Kandahar aboard a waiting Air Force C-130. The Marine in the foreground is armed with the M249 SAW and an 83MM Shoulder-Launched, Multipurpose Assault Weapon (SMAW). The SMAW is a man-portable weapon system consisting of the Mk 153 Mod 0 launcher. This launcher consists of a fiberglass launch tube, a 9MM spotting rifle using a Mk 217 Mod 0 cartridge, an electro-mechanical firing mechanism, open battle sights, and a mount for the Mk 42 Mod 0 optical and AN/PVS-4 night sights. It can fire either the Mk 3 Mod 0 encased High Explosive, Dual Purpose (HEDP) rocket or the Mk 6 Mod 0 encased High Explosive Anti-Armor (HEAA) rocket. The SMAW weighs 16.6 pounds (7.5 KG) while empty, and 30 pounds (13.6 KG) ready to fire. (USMC)

A Sikorsky CH-53E Super Stallion touches down on the flight deck of USS PELELIU as it arrives from Kandahar International Airport on 13 January 2002. It was bringing elements of the 15th MEU (SOC) back to the ship from Kandahar. The Unit completed withdrawal from Afghanistan on 13 January, when the Marines turned over control of the airport to the US Army. (USMC by Sgt Joseph R. Chenelly)

(Right) On 9 January 2002, a Marine KC-130 from VMGR-352 'Raiders' crashed into the mountains near Shamsi, Afghanistan, killing all seven crewmen aboard. Fellow Marines erected this monument at the crash site. It displays the names of the crew and is topped by the Raider flag. The crash was attributed to bad weather conditions. (USMC via Guy Ravey)

(Below) A VMGR-352 crew chief aids pilots during ground operations by maintaining a lookout from the observation hatch atop the KC-130's fuselage behind the cockpit. A Raider flag flies from the extendable mast. (USMC)

(Above) A Boeing (McDonnell Douglas) AV-8B Harrier II is launched from USS PELELIU (LHA-5) on a close air support mission for the 15th MEU in November of 2001. The AV-8B Vertical/Short Take Off and Landing (V/STOL) strike aircraft was designed to replace both the AV-8A and the A-4M Skyhawk light attack aircraft. V/STOL aircraft combine tactical mobility, responsiveness, reduced operating cost, and basing flexibility, both afloat and ashore. They are particularly well-suited to the special combat and expeditionary requirements of the Marine Corps. The AV-8B Plus features the APG-65 radar used by the F/A-18 Hornet, along with all previous systems and features common to the AV-8B. (USMC)

(Left) A Marine crew chief polishes an AV-8B's canopy aboard ship. The Harrier is the Marine Corps' principal close air support aircraft, and it is also used as a helicopter escort. It operates from amphibious assault carriers as dedicated air assets of the MEU. A typical embarked Harrier unit consists of six aircraft. (USMC)

(Below) A jumpmaster from Explosive Ordnance Disposal Mobile Unit Five (EODMU-5) yells instructions to other EOD personnel to make ready for a static-line jump from a CH-46 Sea Knight helicopter. EODMUs and other special forces units were heavily involved in Operation ENDURING FREEDOM. The EOD personnel searched for and safed bombs and other explosive ordnance before they could threaten friendly forces and civilians. (US Navy)

Two Sikorsky HH-60H Seahawk helicopters from Helicopter Anti-Submarine Squadron One One (HS-11) 'Dragon Slayers' lift off from the flight deck of USS SHREVEPORT (LPD-12) on 15 December 2001. The Squadron, embarked on the carrier USS THEODORE ROOSEVELT (CVN-71), was participating in an interdiction exercise aboard the amphibious transport. The Seahawks carried Navy SEALs to simulate the boarding of a ship that may carry suspected terrorists. (US Navy by PH2 David C. Mercil)

Aircrewman are lifted from the flight deck of USS JOHN F. KENNEDY (CV-67) during a Special Purpose Insertion/Extraction (SPIE) exercise on 26 February 2002. The SPIE system is more often used to insert SEALs on hostile beachheads. KENNEDY and her embarked Carrier Air Wing were en route to relieve THEODORE ROOSEVELT on station in support of Operation ENDURING FREEDOM. (US Navy by PH1 Jim Hampshire)

AH-1W Super Cobras from Marine Helicopter Squadron, Medium One Six Five (HMM-165) warm up on the flight deck of USS BON HOMME RICHARD at dawn on 4 March 2002. The helicopters – part of the 13th MEU's Aviation Combat Element – were preparing to launch on a close air support mission during Operation ANACONDA – the US-led effort to destroy remaining Taliban and al-Qaeda elements in eastern Afghanistan. BON HOMME RICHARD operated in the Indian Ocean during ENDURING FREEDOM. (USN)

A Landing Craft Air Cushion (LCAC) hovercraft of Assault Craft Unit Four (ACU-4) prepares to leave a Pakistani beach on 23 January 2002. It is loaded with US sailors and Marines returning from Kandahar to ships of the USS BATAAN (LHD-5) Amphibious Ready Group. The LCAC can carry a 60 ton (54.4 MT) payload (up to 75 tons/68 MT in an overload condition) at speeds over 40 knots (46.1 MPH/74.1 KMH). (US Navy by CPH Johnny Bivera)

An LCAC carries Marines across the Arabian Sea to Pakistan on 1 December 2001. These Marines were the Composite Anti-Armor Team and Light Reconnaissance elements of Battalion Landing Team 2/6, 26th MEU. The 25 troops are carried inside the hull, due to the high nose levels on deck. (USMC by LCpl Nathan E. Eason)

The LCAC, like all 'hovercraft,' rides on a cushion of air. The air is supplied to the cushion by four centrifugal fans driven by the craft's gas turbine engines. The air is enclosed by a flexible skirt system made of rubberized canvas. No portion of the LCAC hull structure penetrates the water surface; the entire hull rides approximately four feet (1.2 M) above the surface. (USMC)

An LCAC from USS PELELIU (LHA-5), embarked with LAV-25s, prepares to head for Pakistan. LCACs operate in waters regardless of depth, underwater obstacles, shallows or adverse tides. It can proceed inland on its air cushion, clearing obstacles up to four feet, regardless of terrain or topography. Vehicles can disembark via fore and aft ramps, which shorten the critical off load time. (US Navy by MCPH Terry Cosgrove)

A LCAC's craftmaster (right) coordinates controls with his engineer as they prepare to off-load 26th MEU Marines from the USS BATAAN on 1 December 2001. Operating the LCAC demands unique perceptual and psychomotor skills. Additionally, sound judgment and decision-making also play an important role with a machine as expensive and inherently dangerous as the LCAC. (US Navy by CPH Johnny Bivera)

A Sikorsky MH-53E Sea Dragon leaves the flight deck of THEODORE ROOSEVELT after delivering personnel and supplies to the carrier on 29 January 2002. Another MH-53E is spotted on the forward flight deck. The Sea Dragon is primarily used for Airborne Mine Countermeasures (AMCM) missions, but it is also employed in the Vertical Onboard Delivery (VOD) role. The MH-53E is similar to the CH-53E Super Stallion, but features greatly enlarged fuel-carrying sponsons along the fuselage sides. (US Navy by PH3 Travis Ross)

A CH-53E is directed to a carrier landing during Operation ENDUR-ING FREEDOM. The Super Stallion can carry up to 55 troops or a 16-ton (14.5 MT) payload 50 nautical miles (57.6 statute miles/92.7 KM), or a 10-ton (9.1 MT) payload 500 nautical miles (575.8 statute miles/926.6 KM). Its range is extended by aerial refueling through the probe mounted on the starboard nose. The Marines use CH-53Es for transporting troops and materiel during amphibious assaults and for recovering damaged equipment. (US Navy)

A Marine CH-53E Super Stallion hovers above an aircraft carrier's flight deck, with a tractor slung under the fuselage. A deck crewman directs the pilot as the helicopter lowers its cargo onto the deck. The Super Stallion can carry an external load of 36,000 pounds (16,329.6 KG) using two lifting hooks mounted on the aircraft's undersurface. A 650 gallon (2460.5 L) external fuel tank is placed beside each of the two fuselage sponsons. An in-flight refueling probe is mounted on the starboard nose side. (US Navy)

A SH-60F Ocean Hawk flies near the carrier USS CARL VINSON (CVN-70) on 8 October 2001. This variant of the SH-60B Seahawk is equipped to provide inner zone antisubmarine defense of a carrier battle group. It has a secondary 'plane guard' role of providing search and rescue during carrier flight operations. (US Navy by PH1 Greg Messier)

US Navy SEALs practice vertical insertion techniques on the flight deck of the carrier USS ENTERPRISE (CVN-65) on 18 October 2001. The SEALs descend from an SH-60F Ocean Hawk of Helicopter Anti-Submarine Squadron Three (HS-3) 'Tridents.' (US Navy by PHAA Lance H. Mayhew, Jr.)

A Chief Aviation Warfare Systems Operator (CAWSO) aboard an HH-60H Seahawk scans the horizon above CARL VINSON. He is seated in the side doorway behind his .50 caliber (12.7mm) M2 machine gun. The HH-60H is optimized for both the combat search and rescue and SEAL insertion roles. (US Navy by CPH Daniel E. Smith)

Marines of the 15th MEU perform routine maintenance on a CH-53E Super Stallion at a forward base near Kandahar, Afghanistan on 2 December 2001. An access panel is opened on a General Electric T64-GE-416 turboshaft engine beside the main rotor mast. A truck is parked near the helicopter's nose, while other equipment is placed to the Super Stallion's port side. The 15th and 26th MEUs deployed from Camp Pendleton, California for Operation ENDURING FREE-DOM. (US Navy by MCPH Terry Cosgrove)

A Canadian Forces CH-124 (SH-3) Sea King (12416) lifts a search and rescue swimmer from the water during practice recovery operations on 9 January 2002. The swimmer is seated in a basket, which is winched up to the helicopter. This CH-124 operated with Canadian warships assigned to the USS BATAAN's group. Canada's participation in the war against terrorism is code named Operation APOLLO. (US Navy by PH2 Jimmy Lee)

An SH-60F assigned to HS-8 'Eightballers' flies 'plane guard' for the carrier USS JOHN C. STENNIS (CVN-71) on 25 January 2002. 'Plane guards' provide area surveillance near the carrier and Search and Rescue (SAR) in the event an aviator goes into the water during flight operations. It also performs SAR for ship's crewmembers falling overboard. A 120 gallon (454.2 L) fuel tank is mounted on the port stores rack. (US Navy by PHA Tina Lamb)

A Flight Director signals the pilot of a MH-53E Sea Dragon as it leaves THEODORE ROOSEVELT's deck during a VOD mission. The MH-53E has a gross weight of 73,000 pounds (33,112.8 KG). Three 4380 SHP T64-GE-416/416A turboshaft engines supply power. The Sea Dragon has a maximum unrefueled range of 480 nautical miles (552.7 statute miles/889.5 KM) and a top speed of 150 knots (172.7 MPH/278 KMH). (US Navy by PH3 Travis Ross)

The USS ESSEX (LHD-2) is underway en route to the Arabian Sea. ESSEX is the second of the seven WASP Class vessels – the largest amphibious ships in the world – and was commissioned on 17 October 1992. It was part of the Amphibious Ready Group (ARG) of the KITTY HAWK (CV-63) Battle Group. The ARG also included the dock landing ship FORT McHENRY (LSD-43) and the amphibious transport JUNEAU (LPD-10). The 31st MEU was the Marine component of this ARG. (US Navy)

(Left) Two SH-60s are spotted on the aft flight deck of the amphibious transport USS SHREVEPORT (LPD-12) in the Arabian Sea. The well deck gate is opened to reveal the 168 foot (51.2 M) long by 50 foot (15.2 M) wide docking well. This well can accommodate two Landing Craft Air Cushion (LCACs), 24 AAV-7 amphibious tractors, or up to four conventional landing craft. LPDs transport and launch amphibious craft and vehicles with their crews and embark personnel in amphibious assault operations. (US Navy)

(Below Left) Flight Directors aboard ESSEX direct an AV-8B Harrier II as it lands on the amphibious assault ship on 20 October 2001. The Harrier was recovering from a close support mission over Afghanistan. (US Navy by PHA (AW) Clover B. Christensen)

(Below) Two 15th MEU (SOC) Marines service an AV-8B in the hangar bay of USS PELELIU (LHA-5) on 23 November 2001. Six Harriers are typically deployed aboard amphibious assault ships to help provide air cover for the MEU. (US Marine Corps by LCpl Matthew J. Decker)

PELELIU anchors for well deck operations in which amphibious vehicles and/or landing craft (including LCACs) may be launched from the ship's well. PELELIU led the ARG of the CARL VINSON Battle Group in the Arabian Sea. Other ships in the ARG included the amphibious transport USS DUBUQUE (LPD-8) and the dock landing ship USS COMSTOCK (LSD-45). The 15th MEU was embarked on PELELIU's ARG. (US Navy by PH3 Ryan M. Kitchell)

Ordnance technicians load two Laser Guided Bombs (LGB) onto the starboard wing pylon of an AV-8B for a mission against Taliban positions. The Harrier II can carry up to 13,000 pounds (5896.8 KG) of conventional ordnance, including LGBs, 'dumb' bombs, Cluster Bomb Units (CBUs), and rockets. (US Navy)

Capt Jason R. Maddocks, a 15th MEU (SOC) pilot, inspects 500 pound (226.8 KG) bombs loaded onto the port wing pylons of his AV-8B prior to a mission on 2 November 2001. The MEU was deployed aboard PELELIU for Operation ENDURING FREEDOM. Two yellow rings on the bombs' noses indicate the fire-resistant coating applied to bombs used by Navy and Marine aircraft. (USMC by Sgt Joseph R. Chenelly)

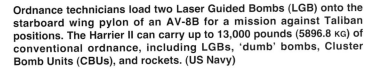

An Aviation Boatswain's Mate signals for the launch of an AV-8B from USS BATAAN for a mission over Afghanistan on 8 January 2002. Two 300 gallon (1135.6 L) fuel tanks are mounted on the inboard wing pylons, while 1000 pound (453.6 KG) GBU-16 LGBs are mounted outboard. A Forward Looking Infra-Red (FLIR) unit is mounted on the upper nose of this night attack capable AV-8B (US Navy by PH3 John Taucher)

USS ENTERPRISE (CVN-65) steams in the Arabian Sea. The ENTERPRISE Battle Group was in the Arabian Sea when the terrorist attacks occurred on 11 September 2001. This allowed the Group to rapidly respond when Operation ENDURING FREEDOM began. This Battle Group included the cruiser PHILIPPINE SEA (CG-58), the destroyers McFAUL (DDG-74) and NICHOLSON (DD-982), the replenishment oiler JOHN ERICSSON (T-AO-194), the support ship ARCTIC (AOE-8), and the submarines JACKSONVILLE (SSN-699) and PROVIDENCE (SSN-719). (US Navy by PH3 Douglas Pearlman)

USS BATAAN (LHD-5) cruises in the Arabian Sea on 30 November 2001. She embarked the Marines of the 26th Marine Expeditionary Unit (MEU) for Operation ENDURING FREEDOM. BATAAN and other amphibious assault ships are assigned a Marine Helicopter Squadron, Medium (HMM) during a cruise. This composite unit typically consists of 12 CH-46Es, four CH-53Es, four AH-1Ws, three UH-1Ns, and six AV-8Bs. (US Navy by PH1 David C. Mercil)

(Left) The SPRUANCE class destroyer USS O'BRIEN (DD-975) cruises off the starboard side of USS CARL VINSON (CVN-70) in the Arabian Sea during the fall of 2001. A CH-46 Sea Knight with cargo slung under its fuselage hovers above O'BRIEN's flight deck. The destroyer was assigned to the CARL VINSON Battle Group during Operation ENDURING FREEDOM. (US Navy)

(Below) USS THEODORE ROOSEVELT (CVN-71) steams in the Arabian Sea during Operation ENDURING FREEDOM. Aircraft from her air wing are spotted along her flight deck. ROOSEVELT set a record for consecutive days at sea while conducting airstrikes into Afghanistan. After 160 days on station, ROOSEVELT was relieved by USS JOHN F. KENNEDY. (US Navy by PH1 Jim Hampshire)

USS JOHN F. KENNEDY (CV-67) – one of two conventionally powered US aircraft carriers remaining in service – cruises in the Arabian Sea between flight operations against Afghanistan. A 'one-off' design, this carrier was commissioned on 7 September 1968.

She is currently assigned to the Naval Air Reserve Force, but occasionally deploys with active duty Atlantic Fleet units. This is the case with Operation ENDURING FREEDOM. KENNEDY's home port is Mayport, Florida, near Jacksonville. (US Navy)

(Above) The crew of USS KITTY HAWK (CV-63) spell out FREEDOM on her flight deck on 18 December 2001. The carrier was returning from an Operation ENDURING FREEDOM deployment in the Arabian Sea to her home port of Yokosuka, Japan. KITTY HAWK is the only US carrier whose homeport is outside of the United States. She is the other conventionally-powered US carrier remaining in commission. (US Navy by PHA Lee McCaskill)

(Right) A TICONDEROGA Class cruiser steams alongside USS CARL VINSON (CVN-70) while on an ENDURING FREEDOM deployment in the fall of 2001. This cruiser was either USS ANTIETAM (CG-54) or USS PRINCETON (CG-59), both of which were assigned to VINSON's battle group during this period. Each carrier battle group is typically assigned a pair of TICONDEROGAs, which direct anti-aircraft and anti-missile defenses around the carrier. (US Navy)

THEODORE ROOSEVELT (CVN-71) steams in the Arabian Sea on 17 October 2001. The Navy deployed her Carrier Battle Group to the Mediterranean, and 'to points East' on 13 September. This Battle Group included the cruisers LEYTE GULF (CG-55) and VELLA GULF (CG-72), the destroyers RAMAGE (DDG-61), ROSS (DDG -71), PETERSON (DD-969), and HAYLER (DD-997), and the frigates ELROD (FFG-55) and CARR (FFG-52). They were accompanied by the support ship DETROIT (AOE-4) and the submarines SPRINGFIELD (SSN-761) and HARTFORD (SSN-768). The ROOSEVELT Carrier Battle Group transited the Suez Canal on 13 October and arrived in the Arabian Sea two days later. (US Navy by PH2 Jason Scarborough)

(Above) A Grumman E-2C Hawkeye Airborne Early Warning (AEW) aircraft recovers aboard ENTERPRISE on 20 October 2001. This aircraft was assigned to Airborne Early Warning Squadron One Two Four (VAW-124) 'Bear Aces.' The rotodome above the Hawkeye's fuselage houses a long-range surveillance radar, which allows the E-2 to serve as the fleet's airborne battle manager. Each Carrier Air Wing (CVW) is assigned a four-aircraft E-2 Squadron. (US Navy by PH2 Darrly I. Wood)

(Left) CARL VINSON and the fast combat support ship SACRAMENTO (AOE-1) steam side-by-side during a routine Replenishment At Sea (RAS). The two ships maintain a distance of approximately 50 yards (45.7 M) between them during this operation. The VINSON Battle Group conducted some of the first strikes against Taliban and al-Qaeda forces. (US Navy by PH3 Carol Warden)

F/A-18 Hornets and (right) S-3 Vikings are spotted on the bow of THEODORE ROOSEVELT during a break in flight operations on 14 November 2001. Wings fold on most carrier aircraft to allow more aircraft to be carried on the confined flight and hangar decks. The Navy awarded ROOSEVELT – nicknamed the 'Big Stick' – its Battle Efficiency (Battle E) award for the best Atlantic Fleet carrier in 2001.

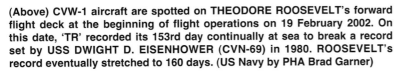

(Above) CVW-1 aircraft are spotted on THEODORE ROOSEVELT's forward flight deck at the beginning of flight operations on 19 February 2002. On this date, 'TR' recorded its 153rd day continually at sea to break a record set by USS DWIGHT D. EISENHOWER (CVN-69) in 1980. ROOSEVELT's record eventually stretched to 160 days. (US Navy by PHA Brad Garner)

(Right) Grumman F-14 Tomcats taxi from their parking spots on ENTERPRISE's forward deck towards the waist catapults on 9 November 2001. ENTERPRISE and her air wing were relieved on station in the Arabian Sea eight days before. The air wing flew off the carrier prior to arriving at its home port of Norfolk, Virginia. (US Navy by PH1 Martin Maddock)

(Below) USS JOHN C. STENNIS (CVN-74) turns out of the wind and picks up speed on 20 February 2002. This maneuver reset her course in preparation for the next cycle of flight operations. STENNIS and her embarked CVW-9 were conducting strikes against Afghanistan. The STENNIS Battle Group replaced the VINSON Battle Group on station on 15 December 2001. (US Navy by PHA Tina Lamb)

Members of THEODORE ROOSEVELT's V-2 division test catapult number four in preparation for flight operations on 27 September 2001. Each steam catapult can accelerate a 37 ton (33.6 MT) aircraft from zero to a safe flight speed of up to 180 MPH (289.7 KMH) in approximately 300 feet (91.4 M) and in less than three seconds. The weight of each aircraft determines the amount of thrust provided by the catapult. (US Navy by PHAN Stacey Hines)

From inside the cockpit of an S-3B Viking, a member of Sea Control Squadron Two Two (VS-22) watches a CH-46 Sea Knight depart ENTERPRISE on 10 October 2001. The CH-46 had just delivered materials from a supply ship to the carrier during a Vertical Replenishment (VERTREP). Carriers use VERTREP for resupply without having to steam beside supply vessels or stopping in port. (US Navy by PH3 David Pastoriza)

A Grumman EA-6B Prowler electronic warfare aircraft launches from CARL VINSON on 20 October 2001. The Prowler is assigned to Tactical Electronic Warfare Squadron One Three Five (VAQ-135) 'Black Ravens.' The Navy's EA-6B fleet is shore based at Naval Air Station (NAS) Whidbey Island, Washington. Four EA-6Bs are normally assigned to each CVW to provide Electronic Counter Measures (ECM) escort for strike aircraft. Signals sent from the ALQ-99F jamming pods mounted under the Prowler's wings disrupt and confuse enemy radars. (US Navy by PH3 Martin S. Fuentes)

(Left) A Lockheed S-3B Viking from VS-32 'Maulers' is readied for a night launch from THEODORE ROOSEVELT on 31 October 2001. S-3s perform a variety of missions, including Anti-Submarine Warfare (ASW), surface surveillance, and aerial refueling. (US Navy by PH2 Jeremy Hall)

(Below) The guided-missile cruiser VELLA GULF (CG-72) passes off THEODORE ROOSEVELT's starboard side during ammunition off-load operations. These warships flank the Military Sealift Command (MSC) ship USNS FLINT (T-AE-32). (US Navy by PH3 Luke Williams)

(Above) An E-2 is launched from one of a carrier's four catapults. A catapult officer monitors the launch from his enclosed control station. The Grumman E-2C Hawkeye entered US Navy service in 1973. It is powered by two 4600 SHP Allison T-56-A-425 turboprop engines. The E-2C's maximum speed is 350 knots (403 MPH/648.6 KMH) and its range is 1300 nautical miles (1497 statute miles/2409.1 KM). (US Navy by PH3 Summer M. Anderson)

(Right) A Marine CH-46 Sea Knight launches from the deck of USS ESSEX (LHD-2) on 18 November 2001. The helicopter was assigned to HMM-265 and carried members of the 31st MEU to shore. Four AV-8B Harrier IIs are spotted along the starboard side. ESSEX and her WASP Class sisters embark up to 32 CH-46s and six AV-8Bs when configured for the amphibious assault role. Alternately, 20 Harrier IIs and up to six SH-60B Seahawks can be carried when the ship is employed in the Anti-Submarine Warfare (ASW) role. The aircraft – selected from shore-based units – are formed into a composite Marine Medium Helicopter Squadron (HMM) for the cruise. (US Navy by PHA Gary B. Granger)

A VAQ-137 'Rooks' EA-6B Prowler flies the 'spin pattern' (a holding pattern) prior to recovering aboard THEODORE ROOSEVELT on 4 December 2001. The Prowler has extended its tail hook, which will engage one of the carrier's four arresting cables to stop the aircraft on deck. The EA-6B's crew consists of one pilot and three Electronic Warfare Officers (EWOs). (US Navy by Lt Cmdr Dave Adams)

An Aviation Boatswain's Mate directs a VAW-123 'Screwtops' E-2C to its parking spot on THEODORE ROOSEVELT's flight deck on 4 November 2001. The Hawkeye had just recovered after a mission and folded its wings aft while taxiing to the forward flight deck. Green vests, jerseys, and cranials (helmets) identify arresting and catapult crew. (US Navy by PH2 Jason Scarborough)

Ordnancemen assigned to Strike Fighter Squadron Nine Four (VFA-94) 'Shrikes' load an AIM-7 Sparrow Air-to-Air Missile (AAM) onto an F/A-18 Hornet. This occurred aboard CARL VINSON on 9 October 2001. AAMs were carried on many early missions against the Taliban, although the Afghans lacked fighters to challenge US aircraft. (US Navy by CPH Daniel E. Smith)

An Ordnanceman aboard CARL VINSON directs a forklift with a pallet of bombs on 19 October 2001. This occurred during replenishment of the carrier's bomb supply following the first round of strikes against Afghanistan. Ordnance crews wear red vests, jerseys, and cranials, although this man only wears earcovers on his head. (US Navy by PHA Inez Lawson)

A VFA-82 'Marauders' pilot inspects a Laser Guided Bomb (LGB) mounted on his F/A-18 Hornet. The aviator was conducting a pre-flight inspection prior to a mission from THEODORE ROOSEVELT on 4 November 2001. The laser seeker head on the LGB's nose focuses on a target 'illuminated' (designated) by a laser designator. (US Navy by PH2 Jason Scarborough)

An Aviation Ordnanceman from Fighter Squadron Two One Three (VF-213) 'Black Lions' finishes loading a 500 pound (226.8 KG) LGB on an F-14D Tomcat. The Squadron was deployed aboard CARL VINSON in the Arabian Sea on 7 November 2001. Bombs are mounted on pylons fitted to the fuselage between the engine intakes. (US Navy by PH2 Nathaniel T. Miller)

A 'yellow shirt' aircraft director Aviation Boatswain's Mate directs an E-2C towards a catapult aboard THEODORE ROOSEVELT on 25 September 2001. The Hawkeye was soon launched from the carrier, which was cruising through the Mediterranean en route to the Arabian Sea and the launch of Operation ENDURING FREEDOM. (US Navy by PH2 Jason Scarborough)

A member of the Air Department, V-2 Division quickly moves away from a VS-21 'Redtails' S-3B Viking prior to launch from KITTY HAWK (CV-63). He signals 'All systems go' to the catapult officer after checking the S-3's catapult attachment. KITTY HAWK's CVW-5 conducted airstrikes against Afghanistan on 16 November 2001. (US Navy by PHA Ronald Gutridge)

An Aviation Boatswain's Mate handler in the ship's flight deck control updates the deck position of an F-14 Tomcat aboard THEODORE ROOSEVELT. Flight deck control crew use templates representing the different types of aircraft aboard to ensure their proper location for each event aboard the carrier. (US Navy by CPH Eric A. Clement)

Aviation Ordnancemen on THEODORE ROOSEVELT watch over weapons placed on the flight deck prior to loading aboard aircraft. An AGM-45 Maverick Air-to-Surface Missile (ASM) is placed beside the white ordnance truck. Several 500 pound GBU-12 Paveway II LGBs are laid near the Maverick. (US Navy by PHA Amy Dela Torres)

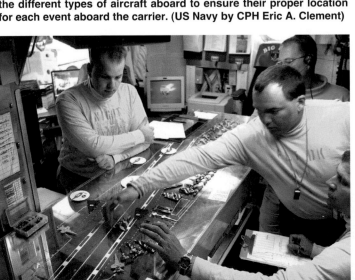

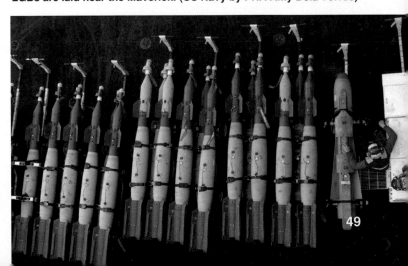

An F-14 taxies to the number one (starboard bow) catapult aboard USS ENTERPRISE on 16 September 2001. An AIM-9 Sidewinder AAM is loaded onto the port wing pylon. The 'Big E' was cruising in the Mediterranean, headed for the Suez Canal and then the Arabian Sea. (US Navy by PH2 Darryl I. Wood)

An F-14D takes on fuel from a USAF KC-10 Extender on 7 November 2001. The carriers VINSON, KITTY HAWK, and ROOSEVELT were on station in the Arabian Sea, flying around-the-clock missions against terrorist infrastructure. The long mission times required by operating from carriers necessitated multiple refuelings. This made it impossible for the Navy to service all of the tanker requirements with their embarked S-3s. (USAF by SSgt Gaddis)

Ordnancemen load 1000 pound (453.6 KG) Mk 83 bombs on a VF-102 'Diamondbacks' F-14 Tomcat aboard THEODORE ROOSEVELT on 13 November 2002. Bombs are mounted on fuselage pylons normally used for AIM-54 Phoenix AAMs. The Tomcat has gone from being the world's premier air defense fighter to being one of the world's best air-to-ground attack aircraft. (US Navy by PHA Amy Dela Torres)

Actor David Keith (second from right), a cast member of the movie 'Behind Enemy Lines,' joins VFA-22 aviation ordnancemen in loading an LGB onto an F/A-18C on 24 November 2001. Some of the movie's scenes were shot aboard CARL VINSON, and the movie's premier was held on VINSON's flight deck. (US Navy by PH2 Jen Byrne)

Aviation Ordnancemen load 20MM ammunition for the M61A1 Vulcan cannon aboard an F-14 Tomcat. The six-barrel Vulcan has been the standard cannon on US aircraft for over 40 years. It is driven by external electrical or hydraulic power and has cyclic rates of fire of up to 6000 rounds per minute. The F-14 carries 675 rounds of ammunition for the M61A1. (US Navy)

Aviation ordnancemen inspect LGBs loaded on an F-14 Tomcat aboard JOHN C. STENNIS on 18 February 2002. These weapons were mounted on fuselage hardpoints originally used to carry AIM-54 Phoenix AAMs. STENNIS and CVW-9 were deployed to the Arabian Sea for Operation ENDURING FREEDOM in November of 2001. (US Navy by PH3 Quinton Jackson)

A Navy and Marine aircraft maintenance team aboard JOHN C. STENNIS services a 20MM M61A1 Vulcan cannon. This weapon was removed from an F/A-18 Hornet embarked on the carrier. The cannon was thoroughly cleaned before reinstallation on the Hornet. The corrosive at-sea environment requires constant attention to preventative maintenance on equipment. (US Navy by PHA Tina Lamb)

An Aviation Ordnanceman cranks 20MM ammunition into the magazine of an F/A-18 Hornet. The Vulcan uses a linkless feed system, which increases the amount of ammunition that can be carried. The Hornet's magazine has a capacity ranging from 1020 to 1200 rounds of High Explosive Incendiary (HEI), Armor Piercing Incendiary (API), or Target Practice (TP) ammunition. Expended shell casings are fed into the ammunition tank for removal after the mission. (US Navy)

An Arresting Gear Officer carefully evaluates conditions on THEODORE ROOSEVELT'S flight deck while a VF-102 F-14 approaches the fantail for an arrested landing on 21 September 2001. US carriers can recover one aircraft every 40 seconds. (US Navy by PH2 Jason Scarborough)

The plane captain goes over final pre-flight checks with the pilot of a VF-102 'Diamondbacks' Tomcat on 25 September 2001. Although the F-14 was mainly used in the air-to-ground role in Afghanistan, its primary mission remains fleet air defense. It can track up to 24 targets simultaneously with its advanced weapons control system. (US Navy by PH3 Travis Ross)

A VF-213 'Black Lions' F-14D prepares to launch from CARL VINSON prior to the beginning of operations against Afghanistan. The Tomcat's wings are swept back 75° while taxiing on deck to reduce space, then are extended 20° for launch. (US Navy by PH1 Greg Messier)

A brown-shirted plane captain confers with an F-14 pilot prior to launch from ENTERPRISE. Plane captains (equivalent to Air Force crew chiefs) are responsible for their aircraft's preflight maintenance and ensuring that maintenance crews rectify problems with the aircraft.

A Tomcat Naval Flight Officer (NFO) climbs aboard prior to a long mission to Afghanistan from ENTERPRISE on 17 October 2001. The NFO – formerly Radar Intercept Officer (RIO) – sits behind the pilot and manage the F-14's sensors and weapons. The bulge under the modex 201 houses the 20mm M61A1 Vulcan cannon's barrel. This VF-41 Tomcat is loaded with Laser Guided Bombs (LGBs) on the centerline stations. (US Navy by PHAA Lance H. Mayhew, Jr.)

An F-14D Tomcat launches on full afterburner from ENTERPRISE for a mission over Afghanistan on 18 October 2001. Two 27,000 pound thrust General Electric F-110-GE-400 augmented (afterburning) turbofan engines power the F-14D. This powerplant replaced the 20,900 pound Pratt & Whitney TF30-P-412A engine used on the earlier F-14A. Missions for Navy strike fighters averaged eight hours in length. Carrier-based aircraft flew over the Arabian Sea and Pakistan to reach their targets in land-locked Afghanistan. (US Navy by PHAA Lance H. Mayhew, Jr.)

A VF-41 Tomcat refuels from an S-3B Viking of VS-24 over the Arabian Sea. Fuel is transferred through a hose extended from a D-704 air refueling tank mounted under the S-3B's port wing. A 300 gallon (1135.6 L) fuel tank is fitted under the starboard wing. The Viking has assumed the aerial refueling duties formerly handled by the now-retired KA-6D Intruder, while retaining its primary Anti-Submarine Warfare (ASW) role. (US Navy)

A VF-102 'Diamondbacks' F-14 prepares for a night launch from THEODORE ROOSEVELT during continued strike missions into Afghanistan. The jet blast deflector raised behind the Tomcat prevents exhaust gases from blowing aft into personnel and aircraft on deck. This was VF-102's last cruise in F-14s, since they will transition to the F/A-18E/F Super Hornet for their next cruise. The Super Hornet will replace the Tomcat as the Navy's fleet defense fighter by 2005. (US Navy by PH2 Jeremy Hall)

An aircraft handler directs an F-14 to catapult one during flight operations aboard ENTERPRISE on 12 September 2001. This Tomcat is armed with an AIM-9 Sidewinder AAM on the port wing pylon. Since Fiscal Year 1994, F-14Ds have been modified to carry modern air-to-ground stand-off weapons. This capability was used extensively in Operation ENDURING FREEDOM. (US Navy by PH2 Darryl I. Wood)

A white-shirted squadron safety observer gives the 'thumbs up' signal to launch a VF-102 F-14 Tomcat from THEODORE ROOSEVELT on 19 December 2001. The fighter was soon launched after this final safety inspection. Well-trained catapult crews can launch aircraft every two minutes. (US Navy by PH3 Michelle L. McCandless)

An F-14A Tomcat (left) and an F/A-18 Hornet prepare to launch from JOHN C. STENNIS on 25 February 2002. Both aircraft were assigned to Carrier Air Wing Nine (CVW-9) aboard the carrier. Two LGBs are mounted under the Tomcat's fuselage, while an AIM-7 Sparrow and an AIM-9 Sidewinder are carried on the port wing pylon. A Northrop AXX-1 Television Camera Set (TCS) is mounted under the F-14's nose. The TCS provides a video image of the sky and terrain for cockpit displays. (US Navy by PH3 Jayme Pastoric)

A director guides a blue-shirt-ed Aviation Boatswain's Mate driving the tow tractor pulling a VF-213 'Black Lions' F-14D across CARL VINSON's flight deck. A towbar from the trac-tor is attached to the F-14's nose landing gear before the aircraft is moved. The Tomcat has a gross takeoff weight of 72,500 pounds (32,886 KG). (US Navy by PH3 Martin S. Fuentes)

Two F-14s are parked on a starboard deck-edge elevator on JOHN F. KENNEDY's flight deck during Operation ENDURING FREEDOM. The near Tomcat (104) was assigned to VF-143 'Pukin' Dogs,' while the aft fighter (206) belonged to VF-11 'Red Rippers.' Both Squadrons were assigned to CVW-7 aboard KENNEDY. A maintenance crewman is walking atop 104 while conducting a routine inspection. A TICONDEROGA Class cruiser steams off the starboard side of 'JFK.'(US Navy)

A VF-41 'Black Aces' F-14 Tomcat launches from the forward catapult of ENTERPRISE. The catapult opera-tor ('shooter') to port of the catapult has just sent the correct amount of pressurized steam needed to send the Tomcat into the air. Other aircraft assemble behind the jet blast deflec-tor before launching. (US Navy by PHAA Lance H. Mayhew , Jr.)

A VF-102 'Diamondbacks' F-14 Tomcat is readied for a night launch from THEODORE ROOSEVELT during Operation ENDURING FREEDOM. Position and anti-collision lights are turned on for launch and recovery operations, but are turned off over the combat zone. Flush-mounted pale green lights are fitted to the Tomcat's nose, wingtips, aft fuselage, and vertical tail. (US Navy by PH2 Jeremy Hall)

A VF-211 'Checkmates' F-14 ignites its afterburners immediately before launching from the number three (waist) catapult of JOHN C. STENNIS on 12 January 2002. The raised jet blast deflector behind the Tomcat is cooled with seawater circulated through the structure. This prevents the steel deflector from melting in the high temperatures of the engine exhaust. (US Navy by PH3 (AW) Jayme Pastoric)

Aviation Boatswain's Mates aboard THEODORE ROOSEVELT display NASCAR paint schemes applied to their towing tractors on 20 February 2002. The near tractor is painted in the colors of the No 28 car driven by Ricky Rudd, who was born in Chesapeake, Virginia, near ROOSEVELT's home port of Norfolk. The other tractor displays the colors of NASCAR driver Tony Stewart's car. Her crew participated in the Speedway Children's Charities, a non-profit foundation dedicated to helping children. Carrier tractors are normally painted yellow. (US Navy by PH3 Amy Dela Torres)

A VFA-94 'Mighty Shrikes' F/A-18 Hornet (NH-400) heads towards Afghanistan on a strike mission against Taliban and al-Qaeda forces. This Hornet is armed with AIM-9 Sidewinders on the wingtips and 2000 pound (907.2 KG) Joint Direct Attack Munition (JDAM) 'smart bombs' under the wings. VFA-94 painted this F/A-18 as its CAG (Commander of Air Group) aircraft, which are more colorful than other aircraft in the Squadron. CAG aircraft are normally assigned to the Air Wing (formerly Air Group) Commander. VFA-94 is assigned to CVW-11 aboard CARL VINSON. (US Navy by Lt Ken Koelbl)

A US Air Force KC-135 Stratotanker refuels the VFA-94 F/A-18 Hornet CAG aircraft on 4 November 2001. A drogue is fitted to the end of the KC-135's refueling boom, allowing probe-equipped aircraft to take on fuel. Colored bands on the extended boom allow the 'boomer' (boom operator) to properly judge the distance to the receiving aircraft. He controls the boom with the help of two 'wings' fitted to the lower boom assembly. The boom operator's station is immediately aft of the boom hinge on the KC-135's lower aft fuselage. (US Navy by Lt Ken Koelbl)

Marine ordnance handlers move 500 pound (226.8 KG) GBU-12 Mk 83 laser guided bombs towards an F/A-18 Hornet aboard JOHN C. STENNIS on 3 March 2002. These weapons were loaded aboard the Hornet for a strike against remaining Taliban and al-Qaeda forces in eastern Afghanistan during Operation ANACONDA. The F/A-18 is assigned to Marine Fighter Attack Squadron Three One Four (VMFA-314) 'Black Knights,' based at MCAS El Toro, California. (US Navy by PH3 Joshua Word)

This VMFA-251 'Thunderbolts' F/A-18 is the Squadron's first aircraft to recover aboard THEODORE ROOSEVELT. The Marine unit deployed from its home of MCAS Beaufort, South Carolina. 'TR' departed the US Atlantic coast on a six-month deployment, which took it to the Arabian Sea and a record-setting at-sea period during Operation ENDURING FREEDOM. (US Navy photo by PH Robert McRill)

(Above) Catapult steam swirls around the launch crew and a VFA-195 'Dam Busters' F/A-18 prior to launching from KITTY HAWK on 14 November 2001. Steam generated by the ship's boilers is supplied to all four catapults. (US Navy by PHA Michael D. Winter)

(Above) A VFA-92 'Golden Dragons' F/A-18 is launched from KITTY HAWK on 2 December 2001. The Hornet is launched at a speed over 130 knots (149.7 MPH/240.9 KMH), reaching this speed in only two seconds. (US Navy by PH3 John E. Woods)

(Below) A VFA-136 'Knighthawks' F/A-18C breaks for a target over Afghanistan on 19 March 2002. VFA-136 is assigned to CVW-7 aboard JOHN F. KENNEDY. The false canopy painted on the lower fuselage deceives opposing pilots. This Hornet carries a varied load of ordnance, including 'dumb' and laser-guided bombs and one AIM-9 Sidewinder. (US Navy by Lt Cmdr Christopher W. Chope)

Among the F/A-18Cs participating in Operation ENDURING FREE-DOM is this Hornet assigned to VFA-94 'Mighty Shrikes,' embarked on CARL VINSON. Two AGM-88 High-Speed Anti-Radiation Missiles (HARMs) are mounted under the port wing for use against Taliban air defense systems. Two 330 gallon (1249.2 L) fuel tanks are mounted on the centerline and under the starboard wing. (US Navy by PH1 Ted Banks)

An F/A-18C assigned to VFA-136 forms on another Hornet over the Arabian Sea en-route from JOHN F. KENNEDY. Aircraft 313 is armed with a 500 pound GBU-12 Laser Guided Bomb (LGB) under the port wing. The Squadron nickname KNIGHTHAWKS is painted on the 330 gallon external fuel tanks. (US Navy by Capt William E. Gortney)

An F/A-18C of VFA-22 is positioned on KITTY HAWK's number one catapult immediately prior to launch. The Hornet is armed with Mk 83 LGBs under the port wing and two external tanks on the centerline and starboard wing. Because of the long distances flown in sup-

An F/A-18 armed with three AGM-88 HARMs is about to launch from ENTERPRISE on a defense suppression mission over Afghanistan. One missile is loaded onto the starboard outer wing pylon, while two weapons are fitted to the inboard port pylon. AIM-9 Sidewinder AAMs are mounted on the wingtips. (US Navy)

port of ENDURING FREEDOM, the F/A-18s were usually configured with extra fuel tanks. Nine mission markings are painted on the nose, aft of the modex 314. (US Navy)

A VFA-94 'Mighty Shrikes' F/A-18 flies above Afghanistan on 31 October 2001. Two 500 pound GBU-12 LGBs are mounted on the port wing pylons, while an AIM-9 Sidewinder is fitted to the wingtip launcher. VFA-94 was assigned to CVW-11 aboard CARL VINSON during Operation ENDURING FREEDOM. (US Navy by Lt Steve Lightstone)

Two Aviation Ordnancemen from VFA-86 'Sidewinders' perform routine maintenance on a 20MM M61A1 Vulcan cannon aboard THEODORE ROOSEVELT. The cannon was removed from the nose of an F/A-18 Hornet embarked on the carrier. The curved chute fed 20MM ammunition from the magazine to the breech mechanism. (US Navy by PH3 Amy Dela Torres)

(Above) An F/A-18 of VFA-82 'Marauders' lights its afterburners before an early morning launch from THEODORE ROOSEVELT on 27 November 2001. The Hornet's lowered elevons help the aircraft climb soon after leaving the carrier's deck. VFA-82 is assigned to CVW-1 aboard ROOSEVELT. (US Navy by PH2 Jeremy Hall)

(Below) A VFA-195 'Dam Busters' F/A-18 touches down on KITTY HAWK's flight deck while recovering on 21 November 2001. Smoke comes from the tires making contact with the deck. Aviators apply full power when the aircraft lands, which allows them to get airborne if the tail hook fails to catch an arresting cable. (US Navy by PH3 John E. Woods)

Afterburners are lit while this F/A-18 from VFA-105 'Gunslingers' safely recovers aboard USS HARRY S. TRUMAN (CVN-75). The Hornet successfully engaged the third arresting cable from aft, which is what naval aviators strive for on every recovery. TRUMAN operated in support of Operation SOUTHERN WATCH, the containment of the Iraqi Air Force, which continued during Operation ENDURING FREEDOM (US Navy by PH3 Dwain Willis)

(Above) A VMFA-251 'Thunderbolts' F/A-18 prepares to catch an arresting cable aboard THEODORE ROOSEVELT. The Hornet's approach speed to the carrier deck is 135 knots (155.5 MPH/250.2 KMH). This Marine squadron was assigned to CVW-1 during ROOSEVELT's deployment to the Arabian Sea for Operation ENDURING FREEDOM. (US Navy by PH2 Jason Scarborough)

(Below) The catapult officers signals for the launch of a VMFA-314 'Black Knights' F/A-18 (NG-203) from JOHN C. STENNIS. The Hornet is armed with a 2000 pound (907.2 KG) Mk 86 Joint Direct Attack Munition (JDAM), which is mounted on the port inboard wing pylon. A 330 gallon (1249.2 L) external fuel tank is fitted to the centerline. (US Navy by PH3 Jayme Pastoric)

A Hornet (NH-314) assigned to VFA-22 is launched from CARL VINSON on 17 November 2001. Both port wing pylons carry 500 pound GBU-12 Laser Guided Bombs (LGBs). During a catapult launch, the F/A-18 travels approximately 300 feet (91.4 M) in approximately two seconds. The aircraft reaches approximately 140 knots (161.2 MPH/259.4 KMH) when it reaches the catapult's end. (US Navy by PH3 Martin S. Fuentes)

A 'pig' (towing tractor) tows a VFA-94 'Mighty Shrikes' F/A-18 aft on CARL VINSON's flight deck on 28 November 2001. The carrier was preparing for flight operations against Taliban and al-Qaeda elements in Afghanistan. A 2000 pound JDAM is mounted on the Hornet's port inboard wing pylon, while AIM-9 Sidewinders are fitted to the wingtips. Twenty mission tally marks are painted on the nose, aft of the modex (412) and the formation light strip. (US Navy by PH1 Ted Banks)

An F/A-18 Hornet moves toward the catapults aboard CARL VINSON. The Hornet is armed with a 500 pound GBU-12 Paveway II LGB under the port wing. A AN/AAS-38 Forward-Looking Infra-Red (FLIR) pod is mounted on the fuselage near the main landing gear. (US Navy by Cmdr Scott Gurek)

Aviation ordnancemen load ordnance onto a VFA-97 'Warhawks' F/A-18A Hornet aboard CARL VINSON. The crew lifts 500 pound GBU-12 LGBs from a trailer onto the port outboard wing pylon. Two more GBU-12s remain on the trailer for delivery to other aircraft on VINSON's flight deck. (US Navy by PH3 Martin S. Fuentes)

An F/A-18 Hornet from VFA-147 'Argonauts' is jerked to a stop as it lands aboard JOHN C. STENNIS. The 'hook runner' standing nearby uses the long tool to clear the arresting cable from the tail hook. In landing aboard the carrier, the pilot aims for a 120 foot (36.6 M) area of the deck where the arresting cables are, trying to catch the number three 'wire.' The aircraft is landing at a speed of approximately 135 knots while the ship moves forward at 20-plus knots (23 MPH/37.1 KMH). (US Navy by PH3 Quinton Jackson)

A US Air Force KC-10A Extender refuels an F/A-18 Hornet during Operation ENDURING FREEDOM. Two other Hornets and a VF-41 'Black Aces' F-14A Tomcat await their turn with the tanker. Air Force tankers refueled carrier-based Navy and Marine aircraft going to and from their targets in Afghanistan. These F/A-18s and the lone F-14 flew from ENTERPRISE. (US Navy by Cmdr Brian G. Gawne)

A VFA-82 'Marauders' F/A-18 (312) begins its launch from THEODORE ROOSEVELT on an ENDURING FREEDOM strike mission. The catapult officer is crouched in the launch signal, while the 'shooter' sends steam to the catapult. The hold back bar – which connected the nose landing gear strut to the catapult – has fallen away and rests under the centerline fuel tank. (US Navy by PH3 Stacey Hines)

A British Royal Air Force (RAF) Vickers VC-10 tanker refuels two F/A-18 Hornets on 31 October 2001. The Hornets are assigned to VFA-22 'Fighting Redcocks' of CVW-11 aboard CARL VINSON. The British deployed VC-10s from RAF Brize Norton, England for Operation ENDURING FREEDOM. The VC-10 was an airliner prior to conversion into tanker use. (US Navy by Lt Steve Lightstone)

A Grumman C-2A Greyhound from Fleet Tactical Support Squadron Four Zero (VRC-40) 'Rawhides' recovers aboard the French aircraft carrier CHARLES de GAULLE (R 91). Dassault Super Etendard strike fighters are spotted along the flight deck's edge. The C-2 flew Carrier Onboard Delivery (COD) from THEODORE ROOSEVELT in the Arabian Sea. (US Navy by PH2 Jason Scarborough)

(Left) A French fighter pilot walks away from his Dassault Mirage 2000D strike fighter. The Armée de l'Air (French Air Force) deployed six Mirage 2000s to Manas International Airport at Bishkek, Kyrgyzstan in support of ENDURING FREEDOM. Manas also hosted Marine Corps F/A-18s and Air Force F-15Es and KC-135s. The Mirage 2000D is a two-seat dual-role aircraft derived from the single-seat Mirage 2000 fighter-interceptor. The Mirage 2000D can carry 6300 KG (13,888.9 pounds) of ordnance on nine external hardpoints. It has a maximum speed of 2338 KMH (1452.8 MPH) and a range of 1850 KM (1149.6 miles).

(Below) An Aéronavale (French Naval Aviation) E-2C Hawkeye prepares to launch from CHARLES de GAULLE in the Arabian Sea. The aircraft is assigned to 4 Flotille (Flotilla), which provides Airborne Early Warning (AEW) for the French nuclear-powered carrier. CHARLES de GAULLE and other French warships supported Coalition forces during Operation ENDURING FREEDOM. The US and its allies – including France, Great Britain, Canada, Australia, and Germany – continue the fight against terrorism. The fight will be long and hard, with much blood and treasure to be sacrificed before this war is won.